# Democracy
## in the
# Digital Age

Challenges to Political Life in Cyberspace

Anthony G. Wilhelm

Routledge

New York and London

Published in 2000 by
Routledge
29 West 35th Street
New York, New York 10001

Published in Great Britain by
Routledge
11 New Fetter Lane
London EC4P 4EE

Library of Congress Cataloging-in-Publication Data

Wilhelm, Anthony G.
    Democracy in the Digital Age : challenges to political life in cyberspace / Anthony G.
Wilhelm.
        p.  cm.
    ISBN 0-415-92435-9 (cloth) — ISBN 0-415-92436-7 (pbk.)
    1. Political participation—Computer network resources. 2. Internet (Computer net-
work). 3. World Wide Web.  I. Title.
JF799 . W55 2000
324'.0285'4678—dc21                              99-059023

*The basis of our government being the opinion of the people, the very first object should be to keep that right; and were it left to me to decide whether we should have a government without newspapers or newspapers without a government, I should not hesitate a moment to prefer the latter. But I should mean that every man should receive those papers & be capable of reading them.*

Thomas Jefferson to Edward Carrington
January 16, 1787

*Nothing is more dangerous than the influence of private interests on public affairs.*

Jean-Jacques Rousseau
*The Social Contract* Book III

# CONTENTS

# ACKNOWLEDGMENTS

THIS BOOK BEGAN AS A CONCEPT PAPER I wrote while coordinator of the Teledemocracy Project at the Claremont Graduate University from 1992 to 1994. I would like to thank Dan Mazmanian and Sherry Bebitch Jeffe for giving me direction, guidance, and encouragement during the early stages of this book's evolution. During this book's genesis, moreover, it was given a big lift thanks to the generous financial support of the John Randolph Haynes and Dora Haynes Foundation.

I presented early versions of chapters at various conferences, including the Benton Foundation's symposium "Telecommunications, Governance and the Democratic Process," the 1994 Western Political Science Association meeting, the Meridian Institute's workshop "Designing the Next Generation of Electronic Town Halls," the 1996 and 1997 Alliance for Public Technology annual conferences, and the 1999 Center for the New West conference on the digital divide. I was very fortunate to befriend many people whom I consider to be leading thinkers in the field at these events, including Ted Becker, Andrew Blau, Jorge Schement, and Arthur Sheekey.

Back at the Claremont Colleges, I was continuing to learn a great deal from friends, colleagues, and mentors at the colleges, including Bill Munn, John Seery, Joel Smith, and Sharon Snowiss. Bill and I would have long conversations over coffee at Nick's Café, and he had a way of always returning the discussion back to the heart of the matter, regardless of how arcane the topic or long the digression.

When I became director of information technology research at the Tomás Rivera Policy Institute in 1996, I was fortunate to work with colleagues who believed strongly in the mission of the institute and in the role new information and communications technologies could play in improving the lives of underprivileged persons and communities of color. Morgan Appel, Anoop Bhargava, Kathy Gumbleton, Maria Gutiérrez,

## ACKNOWLEDGMENTS

Aleck Johnson, and Arturo Zavala were particularly good at helping me see new angles to an issue or problem. I was also lucky to have a boss, Harry Pachon, who encouraged me to pursue those issues for which I have a passion.

I would also like to thank anonymous reviewers at the journals *Policy Studies Journal*, *Media, Culture & Society*, and *Information, Communication & Society (iCS)* for their comments on and criticisms of chapters 3, 4, and 5, respectively. I would particularly like to acknowledge the support and encouragement of Bill Dutton and Brian Loader, editors at *iCS*.

I have learned plenty from my colleagues and friends at the Benton Foundation. Charles Benton, Larry Kirkman, Karen Menichelli, David Weiner, Jillaine Smith, Kevin Taglang, and Rachel Anderson are constant sources of insight and inspiration. The mission of the foundation—to harness the power of communications technology to promote the public interest—is etched in the hearts of each of these people, each of whom I admire a great deal.

No acknowledgment would be complete without honoring those people to whom I am closest. Speaking literally, I have had the fortune of sharing a home office with my three dogs, Augustus, Emma, and Zoë, who call my office their bedroom. Whenever I would turn around to grab a book or answer the phone, they would often look up demurely and their tails would wag. My own callow interpretation was to take these signs as a show of support. At the very least, I thank them for their company during the long hours I worked on the manuscript.

Laura, my wife, has had a tremendous impact on this book. This book is dedicated to her. Without her unselfish support and love, I'm not sure I would have reached the finish line. As this book was going to press, Laura and I brought a new life into this world, Katharine Elizabeth. It is a spirit of nativity that animates this book—the openness to and joy in possibility that lies at the heart of a healthy democracy.

# INTRODUCTION

IT IS A LITTLE-KNOWN FACT that a "revolutionary Vote Recorder" was the first invention on which Thomas Edison was granted a patent. In 1869 Edison freighted his device to Washington, D.C., to demonstrate it to a congressional committee, expecting them to laud its efficiency. The way the machine worked, congressmen needed only to close a switch at their desk, and their vote would be recorded and counted by the vote recorder, situated on the clerk's desk (Josephson 1959, 65f.). Using this ingenious device, legislative roll call could be completed in a matter of minutes, effectively cauterizing dragged-out congressional sessions. Much to Edison's chagrin, the audience of congressional leaders rejected the vote recorder, castigating it as an enemy of minorities who deliberately attempt to gain advantage by changing votes or filibustering legislation. Rather than applauding it as an important aid to expedite the legislative process, its skeptics regarded its very speed and efficiency as a weapon against minorities.

In a large and sprawling republic—in a political assembly in particular or in the public sphere in general—groups that are small in numbers or slight in influence need time to persuade large numbers of people of the worthiness of their cause. The more efficient the means of resolution of political matters, often the less advantageous this process becomes to those who are outnumbered or on the margins of society. Unless these groups have considerable financial means either to broadcast their messages to a wide audience or to buy influence, they are consigned to promoting their issues piecemeal. Thus, they need time and civic space relatively free from the encroachment of incumbent political authority and corporate influence to get their messages across to potential adherents to their causes. Edison's vote recorder, while it was efficient, possessed considerable entailments, not the least of which were the unintended consequences and misappropriations resulting from its application to the realm of public affairs.

The cumulative effect of inventions such as the vote recorder, in which the overall effects of technologies are lost in the euphoria over their very novelty, is witnessed in the development of many inventions—particularly, for our purposes, when they are applied to communications in the public sphere. At the dawning of the twentieth century, an avant-garde movement called Futurism captured the ebullience of the first machine age, setting the stage for much of the euphoria over the speed, discontinuities, and vitality associated with modern technologies. Filippo Tommaso Marinetti, the leader of this movement, witnessed in the speed of locomotives, airplanes, and electricity a transforming energy and hygienic quality that would clear away the debris of the past: "put your trust in Progress, which is always right even when it is wrong, because it is movement, life, struggle, hope" ([1909] 1991, 90). What this faith amounted to was a repudiation of the technologies of the past and an embrace of novelty. In 1933 Marinetti, along with his colleague Pino Masnata, published the "Futurist Radiophonic Theatre," a manifesto exalting a new form of performance centered on the radio. This innovative form of theater featured rapid semantic shifts, spartan language, and degrees of discontinuity that glorified in trouncing established artistic forms, such as theater, motion pictures, and literature (Kirby 1971).

By the mid-1930s, these ideas had migrated to social-science and policy discussions lauding the political potential of emerging radio broadcasting. For example, Glenn Frank, president of the University of Wisconsin, suggested in 1935 that "the mechanism of radio . . . will tend in time to give us a new kind of statesman and a new kind of voter" (1935, 120), one who "must master the art of simplicity and clarity" (121). A more laconic, abbreviated discourse, typical of the telegraph and radio, somehow hails as more conducive to democracy than prior forms of communication, according to Frank, since listeners ostensibly would (with respect to political discourse) more nimbly separate the wheat from the chaff. Of course, this radiophonic revolution has not come to pass, at least in the way its early proponents had envisioned. Public officials and national leaders, rather than harvesting broadcasting to enlighten and lead the public, are increasingly parasitic on media conglomerates whose market imperatives wrench them out of joint with the needs of a democratic society (Derrida 1994; R. McChesney 1997a, 1997b; Schiller 1989, 1996).

Today's predictions about electronic mail and the Internet echo the prophecies of early-twentieth-century Futurists who endowed global telegraphy and radiophonics, symbolized by Marconi's transatlantic telegraph, with the power to usher in a new era in governance. In 1922 the Russian Futurist Kornei Chukovsky suggested that modern life has created the telegraphic person, whose compressed, abbreviated, and coagulated language has resulted in the economizing of the English language "into a rapid, telegraphic language" (quoted in White 1990, 143). Chukovsky believed that it was America that was largely responsible for the telegraphic person in its protean embrace of new inventions coupled with its informal and spontaneous approach to politics. A comparable "Americanization" of discourse is occurring with electronic mail as digitally mediated communications manifest themselves as largely spartan, pithy, or telegraphic in nature. Whether this is an outgrowth primarily of the speed and volume of such communications or of an American sound-bite culture remains unclear. However, what is true is that contemporary political theorists (Taylor and Saarinen 1994), policy researchers (Neu, Anderson, and Bikson 1998), and pundits of virtual politics (Dyson et al. 1994) are oversanguine in viewing e-mail and the Internet in the same light as Glenn Frank saw radio—namely, as automatically supportive of a more robust public sphere.

The Futurists of yesteryear and of today are myopic in failing to see clearly the potentially debilitating impact of rapid, telegraphic language on political discourse in the public sphere—not just the potential dearth of deliberation online but also the line of demarcation increasingly separating participants at the center of information-age production from those persons on the margins. The French philosopher Jacques Derrida has analyzed many of the threats to the public sphere posed by emerging information and communications technologies. Derrida suggests that new technologies are more than just more efficient techniques or means to perform a certain function or task. Rather, they are effecting profound transformations in the public sphere, changes that alter the dimensions of public space as well as the very structure of the res publica. As Derrida underscores, "parliamentary life is not only distorted, as was always the case, by a great number of socio-economic mechanisms, but it is exercised with more and more difficulty in a public space profoundly upset by new . . . rhythms of information and communication" (1994, 79).

Unlike the naive vision of early Futurists, Derrida's portrayal of political transformation is more thoughtful, predicated on the profound disruption of political life by apparatuses such as computer networks and the Internet, not to mention the accelerated rhythms and speeds that inexorably accompany their introduction into society. With the growth of the Internet, for example, the identifiable and stabilizing body politic and its buttresses in civil society become unmoored, the relation between deliberation and decision making is unhinged, and the very concept of the political is appropriated and put to work to service media conglomerates and accumulated economic interests rather than the interests of citizens. Can any of us any longer point to a noncommercial space where the interests of the public are articulated and vocalized in a sustained and deliberative manner, where all members of the polity have at least the opportunity to participate in articulating issues of concern to themselves and their families, without these interests being bent, repackaged, and delivered by political actors on their media stage or by accumulated economic interests that exist solely to return profits to investors? To the extent we are unable to locate these countervailing publics, emerging information and communications technologies—deployed, distributed, and used within today's unfettered market paradigm—pose formidable challenges to political life in cyberspace.

The irony of Futurism and its present-day adherents (to whom I refer in this book as neofuturists) is that they seek, in effect, their own annulment and supersession in a newer, faster, and more hygienic movement. It is at best a reaction to the past and a headlong embrace of the future in the interest of creativity, change, and novelty. In the "Manifesto of Futurism," Marinetti suggests that the current leadership of the movement could last only another decade or so before younger and stronger hands come along and "throw [them] in the wastebasket like useless manuscripts" ([1909] 1991, 51). Of course they will accept their fate willingly, as their "decaying minds" are relegated to the "literary catacombs."

Such a view of progress and the future rings familiar in our own attitudes and sentiments toward information and communications technologies. In our constant grappling to upgrade and augment our technologies, we resemble the Futurists in our almost blind acceptance that faster and newer means better. This sort of veneration of the new is evident even in the attitude of many youth toward learning. Many young people remark that books with a copyright older than the last year or two are out-of-date and thus are not worth reading, based solely on their year of publication, not on what might be revealed in their leaves. Perhaps more important, our kinship with the Futurists lies in our belief that emerging technologies are by their very nature good, able to be put to work to solve implacable social and political problems. Just as Marinetti praised "smoke-plumed serpents," "deep-chested locomotives," and the "sleek flight of planes," we laud information traveling at lightning speed through slender glass filaments as the genie let out of the bottle, able to solve magically the problems of our political system.

The primary defect of this overly optimistic viewpoint is that it ignores the threats posed by the discontinuities between the dizzying rhythm of information and communications transmission and the deliberative pace of discussion in the public sphere. These communicative media disturb democracy, in addition, by exacerbating socioeconomic inequalities and the uneven distribution of technology capacity already prevalent in market-oriented societies. When Thomas Jefferson said that "the earth belongs always to the living generation" ([1787] 1984, 963), for example, he did not mean that laws and policies ought to be altered continuously simply because this is made possible by a more sophisticated version of Edison's vote recorder. Rather, he meant that the fundamental laws of the land were to be reconsidered by each generation. Revisiting the laws was achieved through a vision of republican government, by which Jefferson meant simply "a government by its citizens in mass, acting directly and personally, according to rules established by the majority" (1392). Jeffersonian republicanism is not a repudiation of representative government; rather, it is a call to vigilance lest citizens forsake their obligations and end up with unresponsive and arrogant government, government that works for the few at the expense of the many. Even Jefferson could not have envisioned the sort of rhythm typical of present-day communications. Indeed, the speed at which technologies transmit, store, and erase messages may well subvert the ability of persons to share equally in a sustained, deliberative exchange of ideas in the public sphere, thus undermining rather than reinforcing republicanism. It is this political activity and not the invisible handiwork of technology that allows for a constant renewal of democratic authority and lawmaking.

Of course, there is nothing wrong with embracing tools that can potentially benefit a citizenry in receiving political information and in participating in virtual gathering places to wrangle over issues of the day; however, our age is one in which many persons are overzealous in their defense of digitally mediated political activities, assuming a default position where the amplification or extension of a given practice via new communications technologies is eo ipso salutary. Just as the first wave of Futurists saw hygienic effects in new technologies—washing clean the sins of the past—neofuturists, enamored of progress, imbue computers and telecommunications tools with magical qualities, effecting a clean break with history. Critical of the Futurist project, the German author Thomas Mann suggested during his coast-to-coast lecture tour of the United States in 1938 that societies are highly susceptible to what he called a "painful eagerness for novelty" (1938, 13), the charm of which presents existing states of affairs as tiresome, decrepit, and out of date. Mann exhorted Americans to resist this temptation to reject democracy and acquiesce to the newer, fresher brands of politics embodied in fascism and bolshevism. The charms of emerging information and communications technologies must also be examined critically, particularly the claims that through new technologies American democracy can be enhanced and extended to include more direct forms of democracy. While these new structures are celebrated in the academic and popular press, representing the very novelties meant to reinvigorate a somnambulistic democracy, we ought to be wary of supplying technological solutions to what are fundamentally political problems, in part related to the *distribution* of resources, skills, and the essential means of communication in a market-oriented liberal democracy.

This book aims to shed light on a phenomenon that is misunderstood and hyperbolized in the literature—that is, the relationship between a robust public sphere and emerging information and communications technologies. In particular, I focus on the new challenges posed by technologies such as e-mail, Usenet, and the Internet as they are unequally distributed, misused, and designed to reify asymmetrical power relations. The central message of the book is that rather than being the antidote to democratic ills, as present-day futurists believe, new information and communications technologies, as currently designed and used, pose formidable obstacles to achieving a more just and humane social order in the digital age. As Henry David Thoreau suggested, "with a hundred 'modern improvements' there is an illusion about them; there is not always a positive advance" ([1854] 1985, 363). For example, with respect to the proliferation of the Internet and the transition to digital television, an illusion imbues their relevance to democratic practice. There is often an appearance of progress; yet increased computer processor speed and greater telecommunications bandwidth do not automatically advance the human condition. As long as these tools are universally available and appropriately used to improve what Richard Rorty calls "free participation in democratic deliberation" (1998, 30), then they will constitute a positive advance.

Specifically, four challenges to democracy in the digital age will be explored in detail. First, the barriers to entry into a digitally mediated public sphere are high (indeed, prohibitive for many American residents), since participation requires a demanding set of resources and skills, including the cost of accessing and/or purchasing capital-intensive hardware, the universal literacy needed to manipulate and navigate new media environments, and the higher-order learning—communicative skills and critical thinking—required to participate effectively in public-sphere discussion and debate. The second threat posed by new information and communications technologies is a corollary to the first and relates to the ability of persons to share universally in a virtual public sphere. As innovations in the telecommunications, broadcast, and computer industries supply powerful and multifaceted goods and services to households, we must be careful not to increase unwittingly the ranks of the information- and communications-poor. Without concomitant safety nets in place to ensure that essential services are available to all residents of a democratic society, those persons on the margins of society may fall farther behind the most affluent Americans. The third challenge posed by what Manuel Castells (1996) terms the "rise of the network society" is the potential undermining of the methodical pace of democratic decision making due to rhythms and speeds unparalleled in human history. The question remains: Will quality discussion, debate, and deliberation in new civic spaces be swept away in the current of "scream" television and talk radio, or will these activities survive, albeit transfigured, to serve democratic ends? The final peril described and analyzed in this book is the phenome- non of the disappearance of the public sphere under the pressure of market forces that distort, compress, and even eliminate public right-of- way. Some in the private sector want to abolish the public-interest standard in which broadcasters act as trustees on behalf of the audience lacking access to this scarce spectrum, erecting instead pay-per-use, pri- vately owned media environments in which the public has no legal right to expect free entry.

This book's strength lies not only in thorough analysis of each of these challenges to a democratic public sphere but also in the methods used to explore and to assess these pitfalls. In the first place, the book includes an empirical investigation of key questions concerning the impacts of emerg- ing information and communications technologies on the public sphere. In other words, using U.S. Department of Census information, data from my own national survey, case studies, and content analysis of Usenet dis- cussion groups, I construct a picture of the virtual public sphere that is based on reliable evidence rather than on anecdote or media-induced hyperbole. Of course, I rely on democratic theory to arrive at strong claims to be explored and validated in the course of empirical and analyt- ical research; however, its value lies in its usefulness in shedding light on problems of the day—particularly as these claims impact communications technologies and the public sphere—rather than any compunction to maintain long-lived nostrums for the sake of their age rather than their veracity. These studies are conducted not simply to contribute new knowledge, but to clarify issues for researchers, policy makers, advocates, concerned citizens, and academics who may need to revise the way they see and act in order to restore the public sphere to a modicum of democ- ratic control and legitimacy. Perhaps Thoreau explained this pragmatic vein most aptly: "To be a philosopher . . . is to solve some of the problems of life, not only theoretically, but practically" ([1854] 1985, 334).

This book is also multidisciplinary, borrowing heavily from political science, communications and media studies, philosophy, organizational behavior, and social psychology. As Jürgen Habermas (1990) tells us, the time is long past when a single discipline could interpret social reality with any comprehensiveness. The culture of the public sphere (as it is shaped by information and communications technologies and, in turn, transfigures the development of these networks and systems) is too complex to yield to the interpretive techniques of any one field of exploration. Steeped in the literature of several fields, particularly the experimental design of organizational behavior and social psychology, I have been able to understand more fully how people interact and communicate differently via computer-mediated communications. While experimental design almost invariably suffers the shortcomings of validity (e.g., its applicability to the outside world), its virtue is in correcting many of the unreflective assumptions about cyberspace bantered about by popularizers of the virtual life.

Before proceeding too far, it is necessary to define the key concepts used in this book. The term "information and communications technologies" refers to the important networks of exchange that can either promote or inhibit many-to-many communication in the public sphere. To participate in virtual gathering places or new public spheres—what Howard Rheingold calls "an ecosystem of subcultures, some frivolous, others serious" (1993, 3)—end users must have access to technologies that enable many-to-many communication, such as advanced telecommunications services. Of course, coupled with the Internet and e-mail, these services can underwrite the conditions for participation in the (virtual) public sphere. While distributed, broadband networks are desirable and perhaps essential, ensuring their ubiquity—particularly along certain geographic and demographic fault lines—remains a formidable task. The telephone is an ideal two-way medium (advanced versions of which can supply many-to-many voice, data, and video exchanges); however, the most ubiquitous of all information media, the television, remains more or less one-way, potentially reinforcing an attitude of passivity and vicarious participation in the life of the community. The digital televisions that people will likely soon encounter will either reify what David Holmes (1997) calls the "screen culture," in which persons find comfort and belonging in the solipsistic world of television viewing, or they will use it to augment and enhance their social and political lives. Such a choice will partly shape American public life in the coming years.

This brings us to the other central set of terms used in this book. When

I refer to "democratic practice in the public sphere," I am referring to the sphere of social interaction between economy and state, including the sphere of associations, social movements, and other forms of public communication (Cohen and Arato 1992). The public sphere functions in part as the spaces in which residents of a polity come together to articulate and formulate their unmet political needs. It will quickly become apparent that this book concentrates not so much on formal electoral participation, such as using advanced information and communications technologies to vote from home, engage in national referenda, or contact major political candidates. Rather, the political public sphere represents the vital channels in civil society in which individuals and groups can become informed about issues, discuss and debate these issues autonomously, and ultimately have an impact on policy agendas. As Ian Budge put it, "it is significant that most of the new issues of the last thirty years have been promoted by demonstrations and direct action, rather than conventional political activities through parties and legislatures" (1996, 192). Since the public sphere plays such a pivotal role in providing a sounding board for issues to be resolved by political institutions, new communicative media—if harnessed appropriately and availed of universally—may extend, enhance, and radicalize the role of civil society in reshaping American political life.

The first chapter will examine the relationship between the wide-eyed visions that frequently inform our understanding of cyberspace and the realities that guide, chasten, and often subvert these visions. I will suggest that the generally romantic treatment of this subject tends to ignore empirical and analytical research conducted on digitally mediated political life. More times than not, authors provide a neofuturist or dystopian conception of the democratic potential of new communications technologies, summoning halcyon days of the future or of the past, respectively. A new movement known as technorealism has become popular of late, claiming to straddle the fence between these two extreme positions; however, its brand of technology criticism wields too broad a brush to provide sufficient clarity in demonstrating the key pitfalls and virtues of the virtual public sphere. These normative visions will be juxtaposed to empirical and analytical work in the field. Several of the more important empirical studies will be canvassed, and their shortcomings will be described, particularly their lack of comprehensiveness and their unidisciplinary focus, often insufficient to grapple with the complexities of online political life.

The second chapter will explore and analyze the confluence of democratic theory and vital features of political life and practice in cyberspace. Since empirical analyses will be conducted on the viability of cyberspace as a salutary avenue for political activity, it is necessary to distill its constituent parts for closer scrutiny. These four features of democracy in the digital age are (1) the antecedent resources one needs to bring to the table in order to participate in political activities via, say, a computer terminal, (2) the opportunity to access or to be included in a particular online political exchange, (3) the ability to deliberate on substantive policy issues by subjecting one's ideas to public scrutiny, and (4) the design or architecture of a network or forum in which new information and communications technologies induce universal, deliberative, and robust political dialogue. Since my findings on the whole show that technologies as currently used largely unravel the democratic character of the public sphere, they are framed largely as threats. Of course, they remain challenges insofar as political actors and the public fail to press simultaneously for substantial media reform and for public-interest values in order to realign the aims of communications infrastructures with the needs of a democratic polity.

Chapter 3 uses recent data from the U.S. Bureau of the Census to examine the extent to which a person's antecedent resources impact his or her ability to participate in online political activities. Resource disparities—such as differences in literacy levels, background capacities, skills, and training—clarify the well-documented but poorly conceptualized gap in technology access between so-called information and telecommunications haves and have-nots. Telecommunications policy does not address seriously the resources one brings to the table beyond attention to what ratepayers or service customers can afford. This chapter will describe noneconomic factors—such as attitudes, culture, gender, and ethnicity—that may explain unequal participation in cyberspace's political forums.

Chapter 4 will explore the issue of (universal) access to new information and communications technologies. An argument will be made for reconceptualizing the distinction between information and telecommunications haves and have-nots that prevails in the popular and academic press. Rather than viewing the information underclass as an undifferentiated group, I provide a new theoretical framework—bolstered with empirical data—for a segmented underclass, one in which each subdivision is defined as existing at various stages along the periphery of the information society. A more appropriate reconceptualization of information and telecommunications poverty can assist policy makers in initiating programs that can address specific needs rather than one-size-fits-all remedies. Of particular concern in this chapter is a group that is acutely marginalized from the benefits of advanced communications technologies, a group I label "immune to progress" to underscore the intractability of its situation within an unequal social order. Above all, the persistence of this underclass in an affluent society illustrates the enduring gap between observed reality and the achievement of true human progress.

In chapter 5 I investigate the extent to which Usenet political forums are deliberative—that is, provide spaces in which participants subject their ideas and arguments to a reflective public. A content analysis is conducted of a random sample of postings to Usenet newsgroups with political themes to ascertain the extent to which they are being used for democratic deliberation. The data show that these gathering places are in general home to an array of overlapping, short-lived conversations, usually among like-minded individuals. Sustained deliberation is rare in these forums, which means that, as currently designed and used, they may not be effective sounding boards for solving problems, engaging in collective action, and articulating issues to be addressed by government.

In chapter 6 I will examine how the design and likely deployment of home-based telecommunications environments present new challenges to achieving a democratic public sphere of communications. With the inception of digital broadcast television, as well as broadband connectivity to the home, arises the possibility of developing noncommercial channels to expand the public sphere and to enhance the delivery of high-quality, diverse political and educational content, what we might call "digital green spaces." Yet the downsides of these market innovations are formidable. First, industry's bypassing of communities of color, central cities, and rural areas in the provision of certain advanced services bodes ill for the underprivileged. Also, the absence of public right-of-way or noncommercial space on these networks diminishes the possibility of diverse sources having their voices heard. An alternative to home-based access to essential information and communications services is public workstations installed in familiar institutions, such as community centers and libraries, a concept that stems from the Clinton administration's National Information Infrastructure initiative. This substitution will be analyzed, particularly the potential to relegate an underclass to public access to political information and participation, effectively reifying two tiers of political incorporation.

Four public-policy "renovations" will be described in chapter 7, each of which addresses one of the features of virtual political life described in chapters 3 through 6. These recommendations are meant to help us go beyond the well-worn discourse that has hamstrung communications policy discussions over the past decade. Unless comprehensive redistributive policies are enacted to spread the social benefits afforded users of information and communications technologies, inequality, poverty, and social exclusion will likely continue to blight the landscape of American society in the coming years. If a public-policy orientation is not promoted that redefines progress in this arena as in part ensuring that the worst-off in American society can reap the fruits of today's economic, social, and political life, then the specter arises of those persons already advantaged in setting the political agenda having their power and influence further amplified.

The concluding chapter will outline a two-tiered approach to meet the challenges to a democratic cyberspace in the coming years. A distinction will be made between the important sociopolitical *movements*—aimed at transforming societal values and discourse in civil society vis-à-vis the entrenched telecommunications paradigm—and specific *campaigns and strategies* leading to more just, compassionate, and egalitarian legislative and policy outcomes. Jacques Derrida's (1994) notion of the New International as a new movement across borders and identities will be appropriated to provide a point of departure for negotiating the rifts in technological access, inequality, and social injustice that upset the political balance between groups in the United States and across the world. This critique of unfettered market values will be supplemented by recommendations for sociopolitical campaigns and strategies as well as for promoting public-interest values. Palpable policy goals will be articulated to which participants in the public sphere can direct their energies in influencing both norms in civil society and the legislative agenda in political society.

My hope is that we will take a harder look at the (political) purposes and ends ascribed to emerging information and communications technologies in an unequal social order. My intention is not to side with the followers of Henry David Thoreau and Neil Postman who see in new inventions a giant step backward for human happiness. However, when these tools are used inappropriately and are accessible only to the few, then there is an appearance of progress that reflects our propensity to furnish technological solutions to overcome political problems. If the threats to a democratic public sphere are to be allayed, then the public as well as our leaders will need to know precisely what is occurring today with the colonization of public spaces—including the virtual world—and they must act on this knowledge to salvage these spaces as vital channels to foster autonomous public communication in the years to come.

# 1

# Cyberdemocracy's
# "Troubled and Frothy Surface"

IF EDMUND BURKE HAD BELIEVED the French Revolution was happening at too dizzying a pace for critical reflection, he would never have written what amounts to one of the clearest and most prescient analyses of its deficiencies. In his *Reflections on the Revolution in France*, Burke observes:

> When I see the spirit of liberty in action, I see a strong principle at work; and this, for a while, is all I can possibly know of it. The wild gas, the fixed air, is plainly broken loose: but we ought to suspend our judgment until the first effervescence is a little subsided, till the liquor is cleared, and until we see something deeper than the agitation of a troubled and frothy surface. ([1790] 1987, 8)

This passage strikes the contemporary reader as déjà vu in our experiences with information and communications technology prognostication. Regardless of which way we turn—in policy circles, newspapers, or television—pundits and gurus of cyberspace are lavishly speculating on technology effects, often based on a tenuous grip of empirical evidence. Michael Benedikt suggests a more cautious approach: "before dedicating significant resources to creating cyberspace, we should want to know how might it look, how might we get around in it, and, most importantly, what might we usefully do there" (1991, 119).

Today, both supporters and detractors of the so-called information or communications revolution ignore Burke's advice to "suspend our judgment" or to proceed cautiously; instead, they read only the "troubled and frothy surface" of cyberspace. The neofuturists, as described in the introduction, champion the brave new world of cyberspace, while ignoring historical precedent or underlying currents that might shed considerable light on where digitally mediated public life is heading. Such neofuturists as Nicholas Negroponte (1995) and Esther Dyson (1997) are more interested in the stupefying consequences of "Web years" or are too smitten with "being digital" to notice the trenchant social and economic obstacles impeding our realization of a truly democratic and interconnected national or global information infrastructure. The dystopians are also too impatient to wait until the effervescence of cyberspace has subsided before they speculate on what they perceive as detrimental and ostensibly retrograde information technologies. Benjamin Barber (1998) suggests that virtual life resembles a solitary bird perched in a cage, cut off from the rest of the world. Such a melancholy and obdurate vision sees no deeper than the surface, perceiving cyberspace as utterly irredeemable.

Among those in the popular and academic press who have attempted to analyze the political utility of emerging information and communications technologies, most fall short of providing a comprehensive, methodologically sound, and multidisciplinary approach to the impact of these media environments on the political public sphere. I have already suggested that many thinkers begin with a set of assumptions about cyberspace that often forecloses a more detailed and critical analysis of its defects and potential. In addition, of those who do use some sort of analytical framework or social scientific strategies to clarify issues related to technology and democracy, most are hamstrung by two of the more generic weaknesses pervading recent work in this field of inquiry: (1) the methodological deficiencies and lack of empirical rigor that undergird much of the current debate on the democratic potential of the Internet and digital broadcasting, just to give two examples, and (2) the reliance on certain canonical works and narrow single-discipline frameworks that foreclose a richer, multidisciplinary approach to cyberdemocratic study.

The paucity of empirical rigor and uncritical normative ideals that some academics and many in the popular media apply when evaluating the relative social and political worth of emerging technologies neutralizes a deliberative and reflective discussion of how novel technologies ought to be applied in the public sphere. In canvassing several recent conceptual works in the first part of this chapter, I will show how normative prescriptions presented by many neofuturists, dystopians, and technorealists are undercut by the dearth of empirical support for their positions. Next I will examine research on cyberdemocracy, describing strengths and weaknesses of existing models. Finally, my own approach will be explained and justified as a critical investigation of four key characteristics of the political public sphere, features to be clarified in the following chapter.

## Neofuturists, Dystopians, and Technorealists

Sampling several of the more prominent works on the democratic potential of the digitally mediated public sphere reveals a field that is primarily driven by normative visions, shouldered by reified concepts and categories that ought to be revised if they wither under the light of a critical investigation of their relative merits. These normative approaches have been divided into three categories to reflect the disparate assumptions many authors bring to the table, often with only the flimsiest of support. First, the *dystopians* are wary of emerging information and telecommunications technologies' potential to disrupt social and political life. Their point of departure is in recovering essential qualities waning in contemporary society, such as a dependence on face-to-face political interactions, thought to be more authentic than mediated exchanges. The *neofuturists*, in sharp contrast, reflect much of the unbridled legacy of the first wave of Futurism: an uncritical faith in progress, an acceptance of novel, fast-paced technologies as juggernauts (laying the groundwork for a hopeful future), and a distrust of obsolescing technologies and institutions as enervated and inimical to creative impulses. Finally, the *technorealists* represent a group of technology professionals, journalists, and academics who aim for the center in the debate over emerging technologies and their effects. Proponents of technorealist criticism suggest that people need to think critically about the role that tools and interfaces play in everyday life. This movement recommends a new form of criticism in which technology is assessed from the standpoint of its impact on human values. Notwithstanding the prudential bent of this movement, its principles are rather diffuse, and its manifestos are unclear concerning what human values are to be optimized in choosing among available technological applications.

## Teletechnology Dystopians

Much of the dystopian sentiment that prevails today has emerged out of a philosophical movement known as phenomenology. Originating in the philosophy of Edmund Husserl and employed by Martin Heidegger (later to spread into the realm of political theory with his protégé Hannah Arendt), phenomenology entails a careful examination of the ways in which we experience the world (see Holub 1991). In his essay "The Question Concerning Technology," Heidegger suggests that humankind currently conceives of technology as instrumental and anthropological. The instrumental definition says that technology is a means to an end, a particular complex of contrivances and implements created for certain purposes. The anthropological corollary reveals that technology is a human activity, the utilization of tools, whether it be pounding a mallet or tapping a keyboard. After presenting what amount to fairly straightforward concepts, Heidegger turns this picture upside-down, asking his readers to consider technology neither as a means to an end nor as a specific human activity. Contemplating technology as, in its essence, something different—a way of revealing or bringing forth—Heidegger shows technology to be a way of thinking about nature as a standing reserve, as a resource to be set upon, ordered, and controlled.

If technology is viewed in this light, then (says Heidegger) we can escape the atrophied discussion in which designing different tools (changing our instruments) or performing tasks differently (changing our activities) will be liberating. Heidegger's critique is not simply that humanity has become the tools of its tools, as Henry David Thoreau might have put it. Thoreau's quip implies that technology is merely instrumental. By performing tasks otherwise, we have the capacity to extricate ourselves from our dependence on these tools through, say, simple living. As Heidegger suggests, the essence of technology "is a way of revealing" ([1952] 1977, 12), what he calls "Enframement," in which nature is trapped as a "calculable coherence of forces" (21). Hydroelectric plants, turbines, automobiles, and computers are clearly all means to ends; yet the essence of these activities is a bringing forth in which nature is seen as a reserve of energy waiting to be appropriated, controlled, and spent by humanity. For Heidegger, to consider technology as a way of revealing would be a great step forward for humanity's understanding of how to extricate itself from its incarceration. To see the essence of technology as standing reserve means that "we are already sojourning within the open space of destining, a destining that in no way confines us to a stultified compulsion to push on blindly with technology or, what comes to the same thing, to rebel helplessly against it and curse it as the work of the devil" (25–26).

Heidegger's emancipative vision hinges on one's ability, as he put it, to think of the essence of technology as by no means anything technological. This is no easy task and provides a rather sketchy portrait of how to act politically. Indeed, the dystopian sentiments typical of many contemporary thinkers highlight the impasse generated by Heidegger's conception of technology. Hannah Arendt borrowed much of Heidegger's understanding of the world in her thinking about political reality under modern conditions. Arendt (1958, 1973) was so disturbed by the effacement of politics in the twentieth century that she likened the weakening of political relations in Western mass democracies to the annihilation of public spaces occurring simultaneously in totalitarian regimes (see Canovan 1992). Describing totalitarianism as a new form of social organization in which human understanding and community are annihilated by the destruction of the spaces that nurture them, Arendt says that "it substitutes for the boundaries and channels of communication between individual men a band of iron which holds them so tightly together that it is as though their plurality had disappeared into One Man of gigantic proportions" (1973, 465–66). According to Arendt, what prepares people in nontotalitarian regimes for domination, for the "iron band of terror," is the same erosion of social relations through isolation and loneliness: "loneliness . . . is closely connected with uprootedness and superfluousness which have been the curse of modern masses since the beginning of the industrial revolution" and has become acute with the "break-down of political institutions and social traditions in our own time" (475).

Arendt's critique of modernity, inherited from Heidegger, links the enormous terror of totalitarian regimes and the crisis of authority in ostensibly democratic societies to what she terms the "de-worlding of the world," the complete devaluation of the earthly spaces which relate and separate human beings and allow a genuine politics to occur. Heidegger's basic critique of modernity, as was discussed earlier, is its transformation in the way the world provides a space of disclosure or unconcealment (Villa 1996, chap. 6). Since the modern world has lost its power to forge a public reality, politics is fugitive. Arendt's cynicism about a genuine politics revealing itself under conditions of modernity reflects a Heideggerian concern that the basic orientation toward "de-worlding" strongly mitigates against such sustained practice. In her chapter in *The Human Condition* called "World Alienation," Arendt laments the loss of human connectedness, which she defines as our share in the artificial creation or human fabrication we are calling public space:

> The rise of society brought about the simultaneous decline of the public as well as the private realm. But the eclipse of a common public world, so crucial to the formation of the lonely mass man and so dangerous to the formation of the worldless mentality of modern ideological mass movements, began with the much more tangible loss of a privately owned share in the world. (1958, 257)

In the ancient world, Arendt proclaims, equality or isonomy was the condition of all political activity, but it was not a function of any natural-born rights. Rather, men needed "an artificial institution" (1977, 30), the polis, a "conventional and artificial" representation of "authentic" political space (31). Within this space, men and women could talk to each other as equals and could persuade others of the best course of action in the realm of public affairs. It is the loss of this political identity and public space (and the simultaneous erosion of private life) that Arendt deplores.

Perhaps Benjamin Barber has applied Arendt's thinking more

comprehensively than any other in his dystopian critique of political life in cyberspace. In *A Passion for Democracy*, Barber adopts an Arendtian stance in reifying face-to-face communication in the public sphere as an ideal, while virtual or mediated political communication is viewed with suspicion. Barber argues that the nascent forms of community developing in cyberspace are abstract and amorphous, lacking the specificity, context, and tangibility of face-to-face interactions. As Barber states, "there may be some new form of community developing among the myriad solitaries perched in front of their screens and connected only by their fingertips to the new web defined by the internet. But the politics of that 'community' has yet to be invented" (1998, 268). The frontiers of cyberspace, for Barber, are new and uncharted, and rather than exploring the potentially salutary qualities of these spaces (depending, of course, on how they are designed and used), he has chosen instead to apply a phenomenological veneer over online political activities. Barber's definition of public—people acting in concert to negotiate collective actions—does not, on the face of it, disqualify virtual politics as a variety of public action; yet Barber is committed to following to its logical conclusion what Seyla Benhabib (1992) has called Arendt's phenomenological essentialism. Unlike his earlier (pragmatic) works, such as *Strong Democracy*, in which Barber remained open to the possibilities inherent in information and communications technologies, the author's growing pessimism colors political action as extremely unlikely via what he derisively terms "anonymous screen-to-screen interaction."

To support his claims regarding virtual communities, Barber quotes from what he calls "a typical conversation" on an Internet chat room. This conversation is replete with prurient dialogue; however, Barber reveals neither whence this exchange comes nor what makes it "typical." Several "serious" political sites pepper the cyberlandscape, according to Barber, but they "seem better geared to serve citizens during elections, and often do little in the long periods between them" (1998, 270). Barber seems unaware of the thousands of Usenet newsgroups, community technology centers, freenets, bulletin boards, conferencing systems, multiple-user domains (MUDs/MOOs), Internet relay chat, and new forms of web-based interactivity, such as Java applications, which allow multiple commons areas for political discussion. While the quality of these sites varies, depending on a number of exigencies, so too does the currency of face-to-face interactions. Their relative merit or worth ought to be predicated on serious investigation rather than deciding a priori what shape cyberspace will take.

What is striking is that the examples Barber uses to demonstrate successful experiments in the applications of telecommunications to democracy are very old and involve local cable systems, quite a narrow sampling of case studies given the recent proliferation of web-based venues and civic networks. Barber uses an experimental interactive communications network from Reading, Pennsylvania, first installed in 1976, to assess the political impact of new information and telecommunications technologies. Choosing a case study from this particular network is problematic, because it captures neither where market forces are leading in advanced telecommunications services nor what community volunteers have been doing over the past decade to develop community and civic networks and freenets (Tsagarousianou, Tambini, and Bryan 1998; Schuler 1996). AT&T's recent purchase of cable operators raises serious questions about who will have access to broadband cable-modem connections and whether these services will be closed to competitive Internet providers, issues raised since the advent of the Reading experiment (Werbach 1999). The other example Barber uses is the Qube interactive system, a full-service network deployed by Warner Amex in Columbus, Ohio, in 1978. This system has come under continual fire as a commercial system, designed to provide consumers "choices" in telecommunications services (Becker 1987). Barber says that "the possibilities of the interactive use of Qube for electronic town meetings, voter education and elections have never been considered, and apparently will not be" (1998, 249). Notwithstanding the commercial direction of Qube, other networks, such as community-based networks and web-based political forums, provide alternative models to the Qube experiment (Monberg 1998), models about which Barber is peculiarly silent.

Benjamin Barber's dystopian orientation is so dependent on Arendtian anodynes regarding the loss of public life and the need to return to Athens that he shines the spotlight principally on programs that seem to be failures from a strong democrat's point of view. Like Jean Bethke Elshtain (1982)—who also wrote a scathing article criticizing the Qube interactive system as a mode of mediated interaction that reinforces privatizing and atomizing tendencies already prevalent in society—Barber relies on a phenomenological argument to evaluate online political activities. Rather than following his Deweyan roots, where experiments are to be assessed pragmatically, contingent simply on whether they work to serve democratic ends, Barber forecloses the exploration of potentially salutary alternative political spaces by reifying distinctions between public and private and between face-to-face and mediated communication, distinctions that can no longer be justified in the face of contemporary norms and political practice.

## Neofuturism

Building on the works of John Naisbitt (1982) and Alvin Toffler (1970), neofuturists imbue novel technologies with an almost mystical quality, revealed in their numerous incantations supporting technological solutions to political problems. Embracing novel technologies as implements of human creativity and progress, the futurists reject the nostalgia of the dystopians who see technology "threaten[ing] to slip from human control" (Heidegger [1952] 1977, 5). In his book *Future Shock*, Alvin Toffler suggested that rather than striving futilely to curtail the accelerating rhythms and speed of contemporary life, we ought constantly to revise and rethink our social goals in the light of revolutionary, breakneck change, what Toffler labels "anticipatory democracy." The opposite of anticipatory democracy is what Toffler calls "future shock," referring to the inability of human beings to adapt and change in the light of the accelerated thrust of contemporary life. As the author explains of the new democratic citizen, "avoiding future shock as he rides the waves of change, he must master evolution, shaping tomorrow to human need. Instead of rising in revolt against it, he must, from this historic moment on, anticipate and design the future" (1970, 429).

While anticipating the future and constantly churning our social goals in democratic assemblies is laudatory, many of Toffler's adherents willfully and incorrectly reinterpret his mandate as offering technological solutions to human problems. For example, Jim Rubens's remarks are illustrative of neofuturist thinking in which technologies eo ipso impact favorably the political process: "democracy itself . . . is due for a retooling to function in a different world" (1983, 59). A "retooling" of democracy implies that the process by which we negotiate differences, explore collective action, and solve problems can be enhanced and improved solely by upgrading the implements or tools used to engage in these activities. For Rubens, amplifying the initiative and referendum process to install a direct democracy is proffered as a remedy for democratic ills, although there is no analysis to determine whether these processes have hitherto served democracy well, whether Americans will prefer to act politically via new channels of communication, or whether the characteristics of electronic forums will be supportive of democratic praxis (Cronin 1989; Budge 1996). Rubens simply asserts that electronic referenda will ameliorate current ills. Rubens's normative framework clearly is misallied with the bulk of empirical support that suggests greater prudence in proceeding with a wholesale retooling of political institutions.

By many accounts, widespread access to advanced telecommunications services, such as electronic mail, will lead to a reinvigoration of democracy.

Richard Groper, for example, provides a theoretical mapping of methods by which electronic mail can be used to overcome what he refers to as "the crisis that presently plagues the American democratic system" (1996, 157). The article proceeds to explain that if only there were more ubiquitous access to electronic mail, then America would experience a reinvigoration of its political institutions. Using such neofuturists as Nicholas Negroponte to support his argument, Groper argues that "being digital" is constitutive of today's salutary political life (167). This causal story of ubiquitous access to technology leading to an expanded interest in political matters on the part of the public is accepted almost with blind faith, although there is scant empirical evidence to support such a lofty claim. The RAND publication *Universal Access to E-mail*, moreover, lists as an advantage of e-mail "more deliberative and reflective, but still interactive, conversational dialogs . . . [leading] to many new social, commercial, and political groupings of people" (Anderson et al. 1995, 8). While there will likely be more "groupings of people" coalescing in cyberspace, it is yet to be seen whether they will be on the whole "more deliberative and reflective" than existing conversational arenas.

Whether it be popular accounts of cyberdemocracy (Katz 1997; Dyson 1997) or more academic works (Groper 1996), a body of thought is emerging on this matter that mistakes the effect for the cause. Rather than seeing advanced information and communications technologies as the amplification of the voices of the socioeconomically advantaged and the resource-rich, these writers tend to view technology as the great equalizer, possessing magical powers that can wake up a sleepwalking democracy. Even many postmodern accounts of cyberspace, laudatory of its capacity "to construct identities in the course of communications practices" (Poster 1997, 221), reveal an infatuation with novel technologies that whitewashes accounts of these selfsame tools' potential to reify existing power relations. This current of thought runs counter to virtually all of the social scientific research in the area of political participation, which reveals that the differential availability of resources—including time, skills, and money—largely explains who engages in civic and political life (Verba, Schlozman, and Brady 1995; Rosenstone and Hansen 1993).

Embracing the latest telecommunications tools is certainly reminiscent of the Futurists and their faith in the liberating potential of the first machine age's inventions. Now that we have entered a new age of invention, the ubiquity of these tools is posited to be directly proportionate to the well-being of democratic institutions. In many ways the dystopian theorists and the neofuturists have romantic notions of the past or the future, respectively. Hannah Arendt's nostalgia for ancient Greece, a time in which political space had supposedly not been encroached upon by corporate power and bureaucracy, has been criticized perceptively by Habermas (1983). Rubens (1983), Becker (1993), and Groper (1996), among others, possess a romantic view of the future, believing that technology will solve many societal problems as it becomes more sophisticated and more prevelant in our daily lives. This book proceeds in a more experimental and pragmatic vein. While normative theorizing and visions of the future can guide our thinking and provide us new ways of imagining the world, they must be tried and tested. And only after they have been tried over some reasonable period of time can we evaluate how effectively they have turned out.

### Technorealists

The technorealists cut a wide swath between "cyber utopianism and neo-Luddism." According to an overview of their core message, provided on the technorealist webpage, proponents advocate a new style of technology criticism that expands the fertile middle ground between extreme visions of technology's potential. The technology critic is to assume center stage, engaging in the (technology) policy issues of the day, rather than relegating such crucial debates to policy wonks, experts, and elites. To facilitate widespread participation in technology criticism, the technorealists suggest that being a technology critic is similar to being a food, art, or literary critic. A reflective, deliberative exchange of ideas ought to ensue on this subject so that we can understand and apply technology "in a manner more consistent with basic human values" ("Technorealism overview" 1998).

Although the technorealist approach is sobering, providing a splash of cold water in a climate in which information and communications technologies are romanticized, the form of judgment that its proponents see as appropriate to engage in technology criticism misses the mark. To compare assessments of technology diffusion and its impact on social and political life to subjective judgments about food, art, or literature is inappropriate, since technology evaluation is not so much about aesthetic judgment than about what Habermas calls "formal analysis," such as that used in empirical-analytic research (1979, 8). When the technorealist asks her audience to seek out technologies that reflect our values and aspirations, it is unclear what criteria we are to use to assess the technology. In judging art or food, persons use subjective criteria to evaluate whether to order the crème brûlée or the tiramisù and to judge the overall quality of the dessert. To assess in what instances computers are to be used in the classroom or to determine what types of mediated environments best promote political decision making contains a substantial empirical or analytical component. For example, John Monberg's (1998) comparative case study of an Albany, New York, freenet and Time Warner's Pathfinder Internet website yields important analytical insights that help us assess trade-offs between a largely community-driven network and a market-driven one in preserving and expanding the public sphere. Monberg's findings—well grounded in relevant democratic theory and informed by research on existing practice—provide a font of new information for citizens to discuss and to debate in the public sphere, rather than basing their judgments solely on aesthetic criteria.

Another problem with the technorealist position is its breadth. That is to say, so many diverse thinkers and practitioners are aligned with the movement that its very message is diluted in the process. For example, if one were to read Andrew Shapiro (1999), Esther Dyson (1997), and Langdon Winner (1998) on the democratic potential of emerging information and telecommunications technologies, the assumptions with which they start and the recommendations at which they arrive are divergent. Whose theory is to be used in understanding and applying technology in a manner more consistent with basic human values, as the technorealism overview suggests? After all, Dyson is a Pollyanna, suggesting that the Internet offers great hope to people who can "change their overall experience of life" by first getting involved online (1997, 34). This questionable argument, if it is to guide one's technology evaluation, suggests that investing heavily in digital communities will pay dividends to real communities and enhance the quality of one's offline life. The fertile middle ground thus becomes so broad that it is unclear how the average person is to orient herself. The "formal analysis" undertaken by informed citizens will have to be more sophisticated than choosing between desserts; however, the principles of technorealism are too sweeping to provide clear markers for citizens to orient themselves. Two of the principles of technorealism—that "technologies are not neutral" and that "the Internet is revolutionary, but not Utopian"—resemble pithy advertising slogans, insufficient to inform opinions on important issues regarding the direction of digitally mediated public life.

## Research on the Democratic Potential of New Communications Technologies

This book sets out to conduct a critical investigation of the empirical bases for the claims of many of the advocates and detractors of cyberdemocracy. As we have seen in the previous section, the normative underpinnings of many theoreticians and pundits of online public life are generally unmoored to supportive research and policy work. In addition to these works, a litany of articles and books have been published in the past several years that have engaged in empirical-analytical analysis, generalizing about online public spheres based on case study approaches, survey methodologies, content analysis, or experimental design. All told, these research strategies shed considerable light on the issues raised in this book. While each methodology has its strengths and weaknesses, as we shall see, when they are applied scrupulously, often in tandem with complementary research strategies, they clarify rather than distort the important questions posed in this book.

### Case Studies and Ethnographic Research

Several excellent case studies have appeared of late, including the volume entitled *Cyberdemocracy: Technology, Cities and Civic Networks*, which examines a range of civic networks in Europe and the United States, including the well-publicized Public Electronic Network in Santa Monica, California, and Amsterdam's Digital City. Although case study analysis can be an effective means of investigating propositions about the future course of cyberdemocracy, they are often ill-chosen, as I mentioned earlier with Barber's use of the Reading, Pennsylvania, community television model and the Qube interactive system in Columbus, Ohio, as symptoms of electronic democracy's failure. These experiments now seem far removed from the numerous public electronic utilities, civic networks, freenets, Usenet newsgroups, electronic mailing lists, and electronic town meetings that are central to any definition or evaluation of digitally mediated political life. This latest effort at case study design, *Cyberdemocracy*, represents a considerable improvement on past attempts and brings the issues and propositions of democracy in the digital age up-to-date in an excellent collection of articles.

The detailed case studies of Athens's Network Pericles, the City Information System of Berlin, Bologna's IperBolE, and the Manchester Information City initiative (as well as the two cases previously mentioned) raise important issues concerning interactivity, access, censorship, and the political culture necessary to market and sustain the network; however, the effects of emerging experiments on the political public sphere remain unclear. According to Roza Tsagarousianou's summary of the volume's findings:

> To assess further the democratising potential and record of electronic democracy projects, the impact of the latter on the public sphere has

to be assessed in order to determine to what extent the latter has been widened and opened up; it is clear that the success of electronic democracy projects will depend on their capacity to support and enable the introduction of new forms of 'publicness' within a public sphere dominated by privately owned and controlled media and the state. (1998, 175)

What this means is that researchers need to clarify the extent to which these civic networks have widened access to political information and the exchange of ideas as well as how efficacious these public gatherings are in influencing public policy. This book takes Tsagarousianou's suggestion, and in chapter 7 a case study of the Phoenix at Your Fingertips civic network in Arizona will be conducted to assess the degree of accessibility to public communication in the greater metropolitan area, particularly among low-income and language-minority city residents.

One shortcoming of the case study strategy is the propensity of researchers, the media, and policy makers to want to generalize to all cyberdemocracy projects based on the findings from a single-shot study. Perhaps the most notorious example of this is the use of data collected by researchers examining the Public Electronic Network (PEN), an information system developed by the city of Santa Monica, California, in the mid-1980s. PEN enables citizens in the city to participate in computer conferencing with fellow residents and with public officeholders as well as to post electronic messages at city hall. The general perception of Santa Monica's PEN has tended to be positive; thus many of the articles and reports based on this case study have offered positive appraisals of computer-mediated democratic discussion in general (Varley 1991; Guthrie and Dutton 1992; Dutton 1994; Raab et al. 1996; Aurigi and Graham 1998). Santa Monica's civic network has been held up as a canonical case study, one in which the advantages of online democratic discussion are seen through the eyes of an experiment that was, at one time, fairly successful in galvanizing political debate in an already politically active community. Only recently has the downside of the Public Electronic Network been articulated. Docter and Dutton (1998) trace the decline of PEN as a vital sounding board for residents, suggesting that due to personal attacks and "abusive" behavior by certain users, PEN has transformed into a gateway for information, a public utility service rather than an electronic civic network. Of course, the issue is not so much how PEN was judged but what researchers do with these evaluations in promoting the virtues of cyberdemocracy more generally. With case studies, we must be careful that we do not generalize beyond what the data tell us about various aspects of online public life within the community of study. Carefully choosing multiple cases and testing certain hypotheses or questions across these cases can begin to give us confidence about predictions that seem to be confirmed by the collected evidence.

A variation of the case study approach worth mentioning is the ethnographic study, an approach that entails describing the *contexts* in which people engage in political communication (Mosco 1998; Geertz 1973). Examining how people take part in politics through electronic communication, from the point of view of the ethnographer, involves allowing for interaction between the interviewer and the respondents, so that none of the important elements of these interactions will be overlooked. In his study of Balinese cockfights, for example, Clifford Geertz pointed out the symbolic relations that went on among persons, interactions that may not have been detected using traditional tools from behavioral science. A limit of this approach is clear: one cannot generalize beyond the "tribe" one is studying, whether it be the Balinese or members of certain virtual political communities.

An example of the ethnographic approach is provided in Hiram Sachs's (1995) study of public opinion formation in PeaceNet, an international, nonprofit computer network. Sachs suggests that studying how public opinion has been formed is overlooked, particularly in emerging online forums, and the ethnographic study provides an appropriate technique to describe the qualities of political discussion on the network. At the heart of his survey design, Sachs conducted interviews of fifteen PeaceNet users, all of whom navigate PeaceNet at least once a day. In analyzing the content of respondents' remarks, Sachs found that communication on the network was cooperative and nonlinear, jumping between topics and conversational spaces. While these findings are intriguing, they probably do not constitute the rigorous sort of ethnographic work that will provide deep insight into the nature of life in cyberspace; perhaps the term "interview-based case study" should have been used instead of "ethnographic study." Ethnography will be critical in the years to come to ascertain the long-term impact of life in cyberspace, but Sachs's article does not provide the depth or richness to warrant the label.

### Survey Research

Survey research is rarely applied to the study of digital democracy. Survey research design usually involves the collection of data from a sample of a population to determine the incidence, distribution, and interrelation of naturally occurring events and conditions. The use of probability sampling can illuminate certain phenomena at a given point in time, although there are several shortcomings associated with its use. First, it is exceedingly difficult to derive a representative sample of users from the various virtual communities in cyberspace, given the fluidity of the medium. Fisher, Margolis, and Resnick (1994) discuss several of these methodological pitfalls in a paper they presented at the 1994 American Political Science Association annual conference. When these authors attempted to post their questionnaire to various political and nonpolitical Usenet newsgroups and electronic mailing lists, it was deleted from many of the lists because their administrators believed that the message should be treated as spam (i.e., a message that is unrelated or nongermane to the general theme or topic of the group). Another weakness of survey research is that it captures one still frame on a fast-moving reel. High-profile surveys of Internet demographics, for example, yield disparate snapshots of who is online and what their numbers are at any given time. Birdsell and colleagues (1998) suggest that web users "now reflect a racial breakdown statistically indistinguishable from Census data for the general population" (33), while Hoffman and Novak (1998) as well as the U.S. Department of Commerce's study (1999) both suggest that low-income and minority households are lagging farther behind their cohorts in online participation than what should be expected by chance.

Bruce Bimber (1998a, 1998b) has given us the best "cartography" or empirical mapping of political participation on the Internet. The author's own random-digit-dial (RDD) telephone surveys, conducted in early and late 1998, produced a pooled sample ($N$) of 2,034 cases, about 730 of which were adults with access to the Internet. Another large online survey sample ($N=13,031$), which ran for one year at selected political and government-oriented Internet sites in 1996 and 1997, also provides a rich data source to tap. The conclusions Bimber drew from these surveys were on the whole rather pessimistic. Suggesting that "the idea of the Internet transforming patterns of citizen-to-government communication or increasing overall participation seems unlikely" (1998b, 30), Bimber suggests that communications technologies themselves have very little effect on citizen participation and political communication. Indeed, what is more likely is that there has been a "democratization of elites" in which the Internet is a new and complementary resource for those persons who are already engaged in public affairs. This process may enlarge the gap that already exists between the politically active and inactive in U.S. society (1998a, 4, 29).

I use census data as well as data from my own survey to reach conclusions regarding the possession of antecedent resources, accessibility, and Internet use patterns. Tapping census data allows me to test a resource model of digitally mediated political life in chapter 3, and using survey data enables me to reconceptualize information poverty in America in chapter 4. A rethinking of the "digital divide" can assist policy makers in developing programs that meet the specific needs of a variety of under-privileged groups rather than blanket remedies.

## Content Analysis

The content analysis approach has been applied to electronic forums, chat groups, Usenet newsgroups, and electronic mailing lists, but rarely to content of an expressly political nature (Davis 1999). Content analysis is a research technique for making inferences by systematically and objec-tively identifying specific characteristics within a text. In this case, the inferences made concern the deliberativeness of online political forums—in particular, Usenet forums whose content is expressly political in nature. By examining precisely what is said and to what extent participant post-ings are addressed by others, we can evaluate the extent to which these types of forums will be useful for the articulation of issues to be addressed by the political apparatus. Lee Sproull and Samer Faraj (1995) examined the Internet as a social technology and have analyzed the content of var-ious electronic forums, looking at users not as information seekers but as social beings in need of affiliation. While this is certainly one important use of virtual political venues, if such forums are to be used to set politi-cal agendas and to negotiate differences, they will have to be designed and used differently, not just as conversational spaces but as problem-solving arenas.

Richard Davis's book *The Web of Politics* provides an excellent overview of how the Internet is impacting the American political system. The book provides a content analysis of three Usenet groups, one representing the political left, one the right, and the last a site oriented toward discussion of a single individual, alt.politics.Clinton. Davis analyzes the exchange of messages, and while his coding scheme is not explicit, he reaches conclu-sions that are consonant with the findings presented in chapter 5. Concluding that the "promise of Usenet is a hollow one" (1999, 167), Davis advocates moderated forums as the antidote to the chaos of unfet-tered discourse. While this is a necessary condition, it is hard to imagine how a facilitator would emerge on a highly partisan website to encourage a diversity of viewpoints, tolerance, and civility unless rules of order were in place to which subscribers consent as a condition of participation.

In chapter 5 I present a content analysis of a random sample of Usenet forums whose purpose is exclusively political in nature. I attempt to ascer-tain through content analysis the extent to which these forums are deliberative. While postmodernists and libertarians have exalted cyberspace as an arena in which diversity can be protected from the prejudice and conformity of mainstream society, they have yet to demonstrate how these venues will support democratic praxis in the coming years. Of course, supporting spaces in which previously assailed groups can find a protective arena in which they can explore their "experiments in living," as John Stuart Mill might have put it, is of the highest priority, but so too is the cultivation of a public sphere that can chasten our political institutions and support practical alternatives to the status quo in advancing a progressive social agenda.

## Experimental Design

The main use of this methodology is to draw causal inferences about certain occurrences or conditions, usually to answer cause-and-effect questions. These designs allow researchers to compare, for example, a group of persons who are possibly affected by experiences in cyberspace to others who have not been exposed to this "treatment." Experimental design allows us to clarify how life in cyberspace affects persons, in terms of their interpersonal, communication, and information-seeking habits. These determinations will undoubtedly impact our understanding of computer-mediated public life as a venue for groups to signal and to articulate issues to be addressed by policy makers.

While experimental design is an extremely helpful means of shedding light on cause-and-effect relationships, particularly the effects of cyberspace relative to results one might expect in a face-to-face arrangement, it is not used in this book. I use the experiments of others to study how cyberspace may impinge on the four characteristics of the virtual public sphere, as described in the following chapter; however, it is often infeasible to find comparable nonequivalent comparison groups that have not been given the treatment (in this case, the equivalent would be a face-to-face assembly, perhaps made up of a similar number of participants, with similar demographic characteristics, addressing similar issues with similar purposes) outside of random assignment to groups. Such an experiment would be important and would provide a considerable amount of information about how virtual public spheres act differently than face-to-face forums, ceteris paribus; but such an undertaking was not possible with the resources available to carry out the research for this book.

## Beyond the Mere Smoke of Opinion

As Thoreau tells us in *Walden*, "what every body echoes or in silence passes by as true to-day may turn out to be falsehood tomorrow, mere smoke of opinion" ([1854] 1985, 329). To go beyond the mere smoke of opinion vis-à-vis the democratic character of the virtual public sphere, this book will take as its point of departure the strong claims of contemporary democratic theorists and put them to the test of what Jürgen Habermas (1990) calls a reconstructive science. Habermas argues that the philosophical or normative assumptions underwriting an analysis of any social phenomenon, such as our theories about democracy, ought to be validated against ongoing social research. Contending that philosophy is the "stand-in" that needs to come down from its high horse and cooperate with the human sciences, Habermas believes that it amounts to a stand-in for "empirical theories with strong universalistic claims" (15). Rather than inspecting culture from a vantage point outside of everyday practice, moreover, the public intellectual must also play the part of a "mediating interpreter" in order "to overcome the isolation of science, morals, and art and their respective expert cultures" (19).

For those who say that advanced communications technologies are individualizing and privatizing and, as a consequence, inimical to democratic participation, Habermas's response is to ask for evidence. Collecting and analyzing this evidence involves what Habermas refers to as reconstructive science, appropriating research from a variety of disciplines to shed light on a given problem. As David Rasmussen explains, reconstructive science is a "combination of empirical scientific understanding with philosophical generalizations or universalization" (1990, 21 n.13). Problems in contemporary society are too complex to be addressed by a single academic discipline or brand of policy analysis; therefore, cross-fertilization is required, an interdisciplinary approach that grapples with real-world, present-day issues:

> Telling examples of a successful cooperative integration of philosophy and science can be seen in the development of a theory of rationality. This is an area where philosophers work as suppliers of ideas without raising foundationalist or absolutist claims à la Kant or Hegel. Fallibilistic in orientation, they reject the dubious faith in philosophy's ability to do things single-handedly, hoping instead that the success that has for so long eluded it might come from an auspicious matching of different theoretical fragments. (1990, 16)

When it comes to the impact of emerging information and communications technologies on democracy, Habermas's approach will be applied. I opt for a multidisciplinary, empirically rigorous strategy in which the political scientist can learn from organizational behaviorists, communications scholars, and social psychologists. This approach does not jettison philosophy and theory. On the contrary, they help us sort our claims about what features of the virtual public sphere ought to be supported and replicated and what aspects ought to be jettisoned or revised in the name of developing more salutary spaces in which to engage in political activity.

In the following chapter, I will describe four key features of digitally mediated political life in the public sphere and advance exploratory questions (based on analytical and normative issues posed by contemporary democratic theorists and lessons learned from existing cyberdemocratic experiments) to be validated empirically in subsequent chapters. One of the virtues of this book is to pose questions that straddle the fence of public policy, communications, and media studies as well as organizational behavior and social psychology. These analytical issues, drawn from a multidisciplinary approach to the virtual public sphere, will be investigated or validated using a variety of appropriate methodologies, since no single method can provide sufficient understanding of the many dimensions of the virtual public sphere. In shedding light on each of these features of cyberdemocracy, we can better shape the future of cyberspace, as policy makers, concerned citizens, and active members of civil society, to ensure that these new green spaces serve the entire polity.

In employing these empirical-analytical techniques, the hope is to develop a more coherent understanding of online political life than provided by neofuturists, dystopians, and technorealists. This said, it must be underscored that this book is not driven by quantitative assessment; indeed, its thrust is exploratory, since the subject under investigation is shifting as we speak. The hope is to provide clarity, to shed light on the democratic potential of emerging information and communications technologies. If theoreticians and intellectuals are to serve a useful purpose in present-day society, they must interpret our brave new world, armed with strong empirical support, and not claim to stand above or apart from such study. Just as Burke demanded more of philosophers and practitioners than to read the "troubled and frothy surface" of the revolution at hand, I suggest that we must engage in innovative research and keen analysis of the virtual life if we are going to contribute to a more considered debate regarding its merits and direction.

# 2
# Shaping Virtual Civic Spaces

ACCORDING TO JEAN COHEN and Andrew Arato (1992), civil society comprises structures of socialization and association as well as organized forms of communication in the lifeworld. As has been stated, the diverse constellations of formal and informal institutions that represent social movements or forms of public communication are what concern us, and not so much the political society of parties, formal political organizations, and legislatures. The array of activities and experiences highlighted in this book include many-to-many citizen interactions in which participants in virtual public spaces voice their concerns in concert and thus hope to influence governments or other political actors. In order to shape the discussion of cyberdemocracy and to formulate questions to be critically examined, I propose the division of the virtual political public sphere into four constituent parts, each of which unveils a vital dimension of these new gathering places and modes of engagement.

The four features are necessary for salutary political engagement. Unless they are given their due as essential elements of a democratic cyberspace, the virtual public sphere will be as sturdy as a chair with three legs. Indeed, their neglect by policy makers, nonprofit organizations, academe, industry, and concerned citizens in civil society will only increase the mounting threats to the character of noncommercial civic spaces as independent, alternative, and oppositionary spaces (Jakubowicz 1994).

The first feature to be discussed is the possession of *antecedent resources*, the skills and capacities that a person brings to the table to achieve a certain (political) functioning. Oftentimes policy makers neglect the building of human and social capital in a community in favor of simplistic yet politically attractive decisions about providing more accessible computers and network connections, without ensuring that resident have sufficient literacy and confidence to utilize the workstation effectively. In the early decades of the twentieth century, the electrification of domiciles led to an increased demand for educated employees, appliance repair, electrical work, and so forth. The subsequent "high-school movement" witnessed escalating graduation rates, enabling those from less fortunate backgrounds to enter higher-paying occupations (Goldin and Katz 1995). Today, with computer literacy becoming essential and the economy demanding a flexible workforce, it is necessary to cultivate a larger portfolio of skills and talents to compete in the global information society. Possession of a threshold level of human capital is fundamental to participate in information-age work as well as online activities, including public communication. As Steven Rosenstone and John Mark Hansen (1993) suggest, for example, "those with many years of formal schooling are substantially more likely to read newspapers, follow the news, and be politically informed, all of which makes them more aware of the opportunities to participate and more likely to possess information with which to do so" (14).

Related to this attention to human-capacity building is the need to ensure that all those persons potentially affected by a policy have the opportunity to express their preferences and influence policy, where appropriate, via advanced telecommunications tools. This characteristic, which I call *inclusiveness*, reflects a long-standing commitment in democratic social orders to universal participation in political decision making. As Robert Dahl attests, "when a large class of adults is excluded from citizenship their interests will almost certainly not be given equal consideration" (1989, 129). With online political participation, for example, so-called netizens are able to amplify their voices on public matters, perhaps exacerbating the gap between themselves and those persons who exist on the margins of decision making, familiarly referred to as information and communications have-nots. As John Dewey put it, "representative government must at least seem to be founded on public interests as they are revealed to public belief. The days are past when government can be carried on without any pretense of ascertaining the wishes of the governed" ([1927] 1954, 181). Universal access to vital information channels thus serves the dual purpose of restoring confidence in democratic decision making and concurrently providing an alternative outlet to express preferences and needs.

The third feature of digitally mediated public life is *deliberation*, that is, subjecting one's ideas and opinions to the light of day for validation. With deliberative democracy, interlocutors in a political debate need to provide reasons to support their arguments, reasons that can be validated intersubjectively in a public space free from the interference of corporate powers seeking to mobilize purchasing power or entrenched political actors attempting to manipulate voter preferences. Many social democrats argue that one of the most important organizational tasks for social movements in the coming years is to weave local decision-making assemblies into the governance process. In order for these groups to act collectively, however, they need to fashion a voice that reflects the considered judgment of participants working in concert rather than just the loudest shouts.

*Design* is the fourth characteristic of virtual political life, a broad term covering the architecture of a network, including whether a network is interactive, moderated, secure, and uncensored, with sufficient capacity reserved for noncommercial purposes. W. Russell Neuman argues forcefully that emerging information and communications technologies lead to horizontal, decentralized decision making:

> The greater ease with which different communications media can be connected with each other, the dramatic growth in new channels of high-quality, two-way communication, and the development of user-controlled electronic intelligence and information processing lead strongly in the direction of diverse, pluralistic communications flows controlled by the citizenry, rather than by central authorities. (1991, 76)

However, the control of these technologies in the hands of corporate giants interested in deploying services primarily to large businesses and to affluent residential customers subverts Neuman's vision, casting doubts on the ability of these tools to deliver on their promises (R. McChesney 1997b; Schiller 1996). In addition, unless the design of networks facilitates open access to information and communications (Werbach 1999), as well as public right-of-way, the power of what Aurigi and Graham (1998) call a "transnational elite group" may be reinforced and amplified.

Clearly, these four features are inextricably linked. Network design is obviously critical to the regulation of online speech—the rules and protocols that are requisite to deliberation. Universal accessibility to forums is also necessary to provide a diversity of viewpoints and to ensure that the voices of the subaltern are acknowledged, though this does not guarantee a substantive discussion. Understanding the new topography or architecture of cyberspace is important in determining how time and space as traditional components of a political discussion (i.e., carried on in a chamber or town hall, in a face-to-face manner, usually with certain time limitations) are subverted within Mark Taylor and Esa Saarinen's (1994) "mediatrix," a place-event in which anonymity, isolation, and asynchronism become familiar landmarks of the public sphere. The empirical, analytical and theoretical investigations undertaken in the next five chapters will require us to revisit the features of virtual public spaces, as described in table 2.1, particularly in suggesting ways in which any or all of them may be strengthened to achieve a more democratic, prosperous, and egalitarian social order.

**Table 2.1 The "Topography" of the Virtual Political Public Sphere**

| | |
|---|---|
| *antecedent resources* | The skills and capacities that one brings to the table to achieve certain functions—in this case, participation in the virtual political public sphere. |
| *inclusiveness* | Ensuring that everybody affected by a certain policy has the opportunity to access and use essential digital media. |
| *deliberation* | Subjecting one's opinions to public scrutiny for validation. |
| *design* | The architecture of the network developed to facilitate or inhibit public communication. |

## Antecedent Resources and the Threshold of Political Functioning

The refrain is often heard that education is an investment in the future of a society. Today's up-front investments, if spent wisely, will yield future returns in human talent and productivity that justify the initial outlays. We hear our elected officials speak of making investments in the future by spending tax dollars on programs on which we can expect a return. The problem with this argument is that, notwithstanding its appeal to our prodigal impulses, it remains couched in the utilitarian language of economics, which places public policy as a supplicant to the persuasive econometric analyses of think tanks and academics. While social science can guide the policy process, it must be informed by values regarding the type of education we want for our children and the sort of society we find is worth living in.

In the 1960s Martin Luther King, Jr., argued on moral grounds for a type of equality in which one's material conditions were taken into consideration in the distribution of societal benefits. Equality did not stop at the door of formal or legal recognition. This argument was a principled one, a defense of equality of starting conditions in which the public sector was obligated to initiate programs that improved the conditions of those at the bottom of the socioeconomic ladder. In his thinking on these issues, King was influenced by John Kenneth Galbraith, who had argued at the end of the 1950s, an era of supposed universal affluence, that unless we invested in the weakest and most vulnerable members of our society, they would not benefit from the creation of wealth:

> Poverty is self-perpetuating because the poorest communities are poorest in the services which would eliminate it. To eliminate poverty

> efficiently we should invest more than proportionately in the children of the poor community. It is there that high-quality schools, strong health services, special provision for nutrition and recreation are most needed to compensate for the very low investment which families are able to make in their own offspring. (1958, 256)

Many of the more recent works on the human-capacity needs of the information society repeat and recontextualize Galbraith's analysis of society, while shifting the responsibility for such programs from government to civil society and public-private partnerships (Reich 1991; Drucker 1993), strategies that are perhaps at too early a stage in their evolution for us to assess their relative success.

Programs aimed at mitigating resource disparities between rich and poor seem to be in decline. The Elementary and Secondary Education Act (ESEA), passed in 1965 and partially reauthorized in 1994 as the Improving America's Schools Act, is a notable exception, aimed at redressing imbalances in educational resources and skills between rich and poor. The ESEA proclaimed that children ought to reach high standards "even if they are from poor families, from families which do not speak English, or who are otherwise 'educationally disadvantaged.'" This principle has continued to animate policies related to building human capital and technology infrastructure development. The GOALS 2000: Education America Act, for example, signed into law in 1994, acknowledged the need for "opportunity-to-learn standards" that will afford all students a fair chance to acquire invaluable skills, ensuring "the quality and availability to all students of . . . technologies, including distance learning." Another means-tested program, the e-rate, delivered over $1.6 billion to supply discounted telecommunications services to poor and rural school districts and libraries in its first year of operation (Education and Library Networks Coalition 1999). Finally, the debate over the American Competitiveness Act that raged in the 105th Congress illustrates the tension between the hiring of foreign workers to fill high-tech jobs and the need to develop indigenous talent. In the San Jose metropolitan area, for example, the home of leading-edge computer and software industries, the predominantly Hispanic public school system and the local colleges are not graduating students with the skills and talents to occupy these technical, managerial, and professional positions. David Friedman (1999) underscores the staggering inequalities in Silicon Valley, a region where the ethnic population in general is not being educated fast or well enough to capture the top salaries necessary to afford to live comfortably in the area.

Addressing human-capital deficits is meant to highlight one of the core problems of participation in American public life, namely, the inability of many among the underclass to engage in public communication and political activities to voice their concerns and needs in their own language rather than having them ignored or reinterpreted by elites. Scholars who suggest that these deficits stem almost exclusively from economic inequalities (Dutton, Sweet, and Rogers 1989; Golding 1997) provide a partial explanation to decipher information and communications technology deficits, but this theory does not clarify sufficiently why low-income and minority communities as well as women are disproportionately alienated from the fruits of advanced telecommunications tools. Richard Civille (1995) and Anderson and colleagues (1995) also focus on socioeconomic determinants and fail to specify the mechanisms that link socioeconomic status to communications technology ownership and use. In the following chapter a resource model of digitally mediated political activity will be presented that goes beyond the abovementioned analyses, acknowledging that it is at bottom the prevalence of antecedent resources that helps us understand the extent to which full participation in online social and political life is possible. If the economic inequality hypothesis were true, then policy makers would need to attend exclusively to ensuring that services are affordable to guarantee ubiquitous access and use. We know the picture to be more complex than this, as will be discussed in chapter 3. Data will be presented showing how differences remain in access to and use of new technologies even when income, race, ethnicity, and gender are held constant.

Without possession of antecedent resources, such as universal literacy and what Amartya Sen (1992) terms the "capability to achieve functionings," online social and political life would be unimaginable. Sen argues that basic capabilities are of first importance in specifying citizens' needs and requirements. "Basic capabilities" refers to the overall freedom to choose between combinations of functionings, such as participating in the life of the community. The question must be asked, What basic capabilities are needed to restore citizens to their proper role as cooperating members of society? Certainly, with the proliferation of computer networks and the World Wide Web, a significant portion of American society remains on the sidelines, unable to navigate these information and communications channels. Ubiquitous dissemination of affordable media is necessary, but people must also have the capability to use these media to exercise substantive freedoms. As John Streck suggests, "the particular role of language in cyberspace may change as virtual reality is refined, but in so far as cyberspace is defined as fundamentally interactive, language, text, the ability to read and write, is and will remain crucial to the experience" (1998, 30).

Attention to background or antecedent conditions translates into the ability to take part in the life of the community by concentrating on the distribution of essential resources as well as the conversion of these resources into freedoms. By some accounts, one of these "freedoms" is access to telecommunications (Pool 1983); however, without the concomitant resources to use this lever effectively, this freedom cannot be successfully exercised. While the Telecommunications Act of 1996 was predicated on the availability of services "at just, reasonable, and affordable rates," other resource requirements for salutary involvement in the life of the community (via electronic media) have consistently been ignored. Supported by recent U.S. Department of Census data, chapter 3 will put forth the argument that serious attention needs to be paid not only to how affordable rates are—although this is essential—but also to a person's antecedent resources and capacities in order to achieve the goals of a more comprehensive universal access, one that fosters the skills to participate in the life of our democracy.

## Inclusiveness in Online Public Life

In a democratic society, opinion formation and decision making are thought to be legitimate when they represent the will of the people, typically defined not as the wishes of a particular interest group or coterie but of all persons who are potentially affected by a policy. To ensure this state of affairs, it is necessary to create circumstances in a society in which anybody who wants to participate in the public sphere has the opportunity to voice their concerns, needs, and preferences. In the realm of telecommunications policy, this notion of inclusiveness is captured by the principle of universal service. As Pool suggests, "from its earliest days, the Bell System's goal and expectation was that telephone service should ultimately be available to everyone in the nation" (1984, 115). In the wake of the Telecommunications Act of 1996 (in particular, §254 and §706), universal service is subject to an evolving definition as advanced telecommunications technologies emerge from the creative forces of the marketplace. A problem with this new definition, as Arthur Sheekey suggests, is that "market demands and consumer preferences, rather than governmental regulations, will dictate who receives digital information, and at what cost" (1997, 42).

Although emerging communications technologies will continue to produce manifold political sites, they are products of an advanced capitalism that exacerbates differences in the use of these public spaces by race and class. There is a growing literature that shines a spotlight on the widening fault lines in society (Castells 1998; Economic Policy Institute 1999; Luke 1998; Roper 1998) and suggests that information technology may actually effect widening inequalities in society. As *The Economist* put the problem in its November 5, 1994, issue: "in recent years the economic forces of international competition and (above all) new technology have gathered strength. In relatively unregulated economies, they have driven down the income of losers and driven up the income of winners" (13).

Both Webster and Robins (1998) and Schement and Curtis (1995) make the case that the so-called information society represents an extension of capitalism's reach rather than a new mode of organization and exchange. Suggesting that "its most important socioeconomic manifestations, the commoditization of information and information work, are the logical outgrowths of capitalism" (195), Schement and Curtis view macrolevel changes in society as reinforcing (while reconfiguring) social relations as developed under advanced capitalism. This view is supported by Julian Stallabrass (1995), who sees cyberspace as "a degraded attempt to grasp the impossible complexity of the worldwide capitalist system." Finally, Fredric Jameson, in his book *The Cultural Logic of Late Capitalism*, suggests that representing the global information infrastructure is a "distorted figuration of something even deeper, namely the whole world system of a present-day multinational system" (1991, 37). These observations are significant in underscoring a central dynamic of emerging communications networks, that some scholars choose to ignore, namely, its complicity with and even subordination to accumulated economic and media powers (Derrida 1994).

In his article "Political Communication and Citizenship," Peter Golding (1990) examined access to communications media in England and found a strong class bias in ownership of televisions, telephones, video equipment, and home computers. Based on his evidence of class disparities and predicated on the principle that the exercise of democracy requires access to a "full and adequate range of imagery and information," Golding argues that our notion of citizenship demands that we "lift the mask" that has prevented the poor from receiving vital information. Stressing that there are two types of barriers denying citizenship—those that are largely socioeconomic (i.e., employment, income, and race) and those that relate to the means of communication and transmission of cultural symbols—Golding calls for research and communications theory that examine the role of power and equality in a capitalist system (see also Murdock and Golding 1989).

While Golding makes an important normative observation that citizenship depends on the free flow of information and access to the means of communication in a democracy, his twin categories enumerating barriers to full participation need to be expanded; this is the argument made in chapter 4. The Dickensian model adopted in much of the literature—carving out a distinction between information and communications haves and have-nots—needs to be revised. As technologies of choice are redefined, as the universal deployment of essential information services is subverted by corporate powers, and as government plows billions of dollars into wiring public-access points, these exigencies must be incorporated into a new model of differential telecommunications access. Clearly, those who are unable to access the Internet from home represent the majority of U.S. households; however, they fall into distinct constellations, each with its own pattern and identity. Do these information sources meet the diverse needs of underprivileged residents, including ethnolinguistic minorities and disability communities, among others? Is sporadic, ad hoc access to the Internet at a library or school sufficient to develop quality skills to participate fully in the life of the community? Are we to expect the approximately one-third of Americans who are functionally illiterate to become successful keyboarders and Internet browsers (Kozol 1985)? These questions stretch our imagination in this arena, providing the groundwork for an expanded definition of information poverty and a rethinking of remedial public policy initiatives.

I proffer a recategorization of information and telecommunications have-nots into five mutually exclusive categories, distinguished by the differential ability of participants in each of these divisions to achieve cooperative and participatory status in the social and economic life of the larger community. If the linchpins of the information society, as Schement and Curtis (1995) avouch, include interconnectedness, the ubiquity or pervasiveness of information technology, and the idea of information as an item of production and consumption, then the interplay between the presence of the aforementioned attributes in the lives of persons and the absence of some or all of these features represent bright lines differentiating marginal groups (see Aurigi and Graham 1998). These five groups, as chapter 4 will describe, are subsumed under three headings, existing at varied distances from the center of the information society's forces of production: individuals who are "immune to progress," those who have "peripheral access" to advanced information and communications technologies in public-access places, and "peripheral users," that is, persons who engage in online activities at home other than searching or browsing for information and communicating with others via e-mail. These categories will be validated based on empirical data from my own computer and Internet survey, conducted in February 1998, a study that validates these theoretical recategorizations with a great degree of reliability.

## Deliberation and Light-Speed Telecommunications Technologies

Deliberation entails debate, discussion, and persuasion in the public square. Private thoughts or isolated activities do not meet the threshold of publicness, because they are not exposed to the scrutiny of others. This conception of testing one's ideas in public cuts against the grain of the body of literature in which the public interest is obtained by aggregating individual preferences (Petracca 1991). If customer expression is limited to registering preferences on a keypad—choices to be aggregated and computed at light speed as numeric imperatives (i.e., market share)—this process falls short of democratic deliberation, in which participants' ideas rebound in the public sphere and are perhaps amended over time due to the weightier claims or more persuasive argument of a cohort voicing her concerns in the same public space (Fishkin 1991).

Davis (1999) and the analysis conducted in chapter 5 present the beginnings of an analysis of online political content, benchmark research that reveals a troubling online political world. If we look to democratic theory as articulated by Barber (1984), Fishkin (1991, 1995), Habermas (1991), Mansbridge (1983), and Rorty (1991, 1998), several common threads emerge in describing precisely what is at stake in promoting a deliberative public sphere. In the first place, the public meaning of promoting a diversity of voices is to allow new ideas and previously unheard harmonies to emerge out of the dialectical discord of the public sphere. As Richard Rorty put it: "This new culture will be better because it will contain more variety in unity—it will be a tapestry in which more strands have been woven together" (1998, 25). This view, more fully articulated in chapter 5, suggests that in order to reach agreement (or to agree to disagree), diverse viewpoints must be aired and subjected to critique. The criteria by which ideas are accepted as better than others include whether we can communicate them and find them valid for others (Habermas 1990). Thus objectivity, descriptive of some ultimate truth or Archimedean point outside of history, dissolves into intersubjective agreement, an arrangement reached among cohorts that a solution at which the group has arrived suits the interest of the group as a whole.

The notion of diversity of ideas and sources is critical to an understanding of deliberation, because varying and conflicting views ought to be made available for public consideration. Privileging diversity and committing to localism have been part and parcel of U.S. telecommunications policy, at least since the 1947 Commission on Freedom of the Press, and its classic statement comes from the Federal Communications Commission's 1949 report explicating the Fairness Doctrine (Kahn 1973). This said, the removal of obstacles to the free flow of ideas is a necessary but insufficient condition for achieving a deliberative political dialogue, whether it be face-to-face or virtual. Agreement among people is not determined solely by the number of ideas that can be vocalized, broadcast, or netcast. While the Internet may be a potent medium for self-expression, it remains to be seen how effective it will be for collective action. Indeed, the public often becomes awash in words and images in the absence of editing, filtering, and facilitation, not to mention the virtues of listening to and cooperating with others so as to articulate issues to officeholders (Shenk 1997).

One urgent issue that needs to be addressed related to the content of political discourse is the status of the "marketplace of ideas" in cyberspace—an arena in which, on the one hand, users can be publishers or producers of content while, on the other hand, their endeavors are circumscribed by private and governmental actors who are, to borrow a term from Habermas (1987), "colonizing" the space in which political discussion can occur. If cable operators, such as the nation's largest, AT&T, are likely to close their high-speed services to competition, then will not subscribers receive information and ideas primarily from AT&T's e-commerce and advertising partners? This growing phenomenon, if not curtailed, will significantly inhibit the ability of the individual to be both the author of her own (political) texts and a reflective participant in the political public sphere.

Few scholarly treatments have examined the actual content of political speech in terms of what is being said, how it is being said, and whether there is a diversity of viewpoints on the Internet, not only between groups but within forums as well. In its brief arguing against the constitutionality of the Communications Decency Act, the American Civil Liberties Union and other groups took as their point of departure the view that "the Internet has no parallel in the history of human communication," particularly in its ability to "provide a foundation for new forms of community—communities based not on any accident of geographic proximity, but on bonds of common interest, belief, culture or temperament" (American Civil Liberties Union et al. 1996). While undoubtedly the First Amendment issues are of fundamental importance in this case, the ACLU, as well as other organizations interested in the free use of the Internet, may well be reifying the concepts and categories that define "community." Does not a "community of interest" already presuppose a certain web of relations that has brought an individual around to prefer a specific interest over alternatives? Do not "antiabortion" or "pro-life" supporters already assume a commonality of interest within their respective groups that the Internet likely supports but may not necessarily transform? In chapter 5 I suggest that homophily—that is, the propensity to gravitate to persons with similar viewpoints—is fairly common on the Internet, and to the extent that emerging communications networks allow individuals to more easily locate those with whom they agree, the notion of new communities is reified. Rather than creating environments in which ideas and viewpoints can be challenged and contested, the Internet may well be reinforcing and accelerating the pace of balkanization, a phenomenon that erodes deliberative democracy and the working out of problems and issues in the public sphere.

Another important aspect of deliberation is that participants in a public forum, face-to-face or virtual, ought to spend time reflecting on the merit of alternative arguments and positions rather than just responding or voicing their own preferences unreflectively. It is often heard today that the Internet is an uncivil environment in which online communication resembles more the sound-bite culture of television or the raucous tone of talk radio than the sedate and respectful discussions said to predominate in small-town assemblies or group meetings (Mansbridge 1983). Deliberation means thinking through an issue, contemplating its advantages and disadvantages as well as the trade-offs associated with supporting a particular issue or agenda. This activity is not possible unless public communication includes taking the time to reflect on issues and to respond to an interlocutor in the public sphere only after sedate reflection on the merits and shortfalls of her position (Fishkin 1991, 1995). With asynchronous communication in most online environments, there is no obligation to respond immediately, as would be the case in a face-to-face encounter in which a person to whom I spoke would be seen as unusual at best or rude at worst if she did not respond after being addressed directly.

The final point to be made is that only through deliberation can an association come to delineate a common interest on issues. Of course, it is possible that private interests and ideals can overlap, perhaps by coincidence, but this would have to represent the extreme case, unlikely under most circumstances. Ideally, through the airing of preferences and the discussion of interests, individuals can make one another's good their own. It is unlikely that individuals in a political forum who simply provide messages and neither "listen" nor respond to the viewpoints of others will change their opinions and preferences. They are interested mainly in vocalizing their individual or private interests and care little for adapting the position of another through persuasion, negotiation, and compromise. These tactics are learned in the process of talking, listening, and responding respectfully to fellow participants in a public space. They are perhaps never acquired by those who believe that politics exists solely to promote one's private interests and that the sum total of private interests somehow equals or amounts to the public good.

Lee Sproull and Samer Faraj (1995) examined several social Usenet groups, dealing with sex and atheism, and some of their concepts and categories serve as a basis for my own content analysis. The authors found that the Net was a "social technology," one that demonstrated that people are "social beings who need affiliation" (62) as much as they want information. According to Sproull and Faraj, moreover, electronic gatherings have three noteworthy social attributes not found in real-world gatherings: (1) physical distance is no longer a substantial barrier to participation; (2) most participants are relatively invisible, with signals and cues limited to ASCII text; and (3) logistical and social costs to participate are quite low. Even though their metaphor of the gathering place is a comforting one, it is perhaps not accurate to describe political forums in which political opinion must serve as a sounding board for the presentation of viable policy alternatives. While this study accords with Sproull and Faraj's in viewing virtual public spheres as fulfilling the human need for affiliation, these forums may be more akin to what Michael Schudson (1997) calls "the sociable model of conversation," oriented toward the pleasure of interacting with others in conversation, rather than toward addressing or solving problems. The problem-solving understanding of conversation is one geared toward the articulation of common ends. Data gathered in chapter 5 do not support the problem-solving mode as the chief characteristic of online political discussion (see also Davis 1999). Indeed, even the social model is an attenuated one when so many of the messages posted on these forums are unrequited.

## Designing a Democratic Future

The fourth general feature of the public sphere is the design or architecture that is developed in order to facilitate discussion. As Guthrie and

Dutton (1992) suggest, the design of a network entails a prior policy commitment to the sorts of interactions its designers want to take place, whether they be officeholders or industry executives. The design modes arrived at via market and social forces regarding bandwidth issues (Negroponte 1995), cost structure (MacKie-Mason and Varian 1995), user interface concerns (K. McChesney 1998), technology architecture (Neuman 1991), and "rules of order" (Dutton 1996), all told, affect the extent to which content can be delivered, end users can be information producers, and less-inhibited yet orderly speech can predominate online. On the issue of architecture, for example, Burgelman (1994) argues that many new distribution media enable consultation but do not allow conversation whereby one can exchange individually stored information, such as electronic mail. For example, cable, satellite, and broadcast television as currently arranged (digital or otherwise) may allow the user to request movie selections or see different angles of the baseball field, but they are not interactive in allowing users to be producers of content and to exchange messages laterally with other network users. The design of these media seems to be more amenable to plebiscitary democracy, where the individual need only register her preferences, than to a mode of democracy in which conversation, deliberation, and critical-rational reflection are integral components.

Given that much of the present-day means of communication are owned and controlled by private, transnational conglomerates, the likelihood that the so-called communications revolutions will include a completely separate capacity or conduit solely for public broadcasting is far from assured. The Advisory Committee on Public Interest Obligations of Digital Television Broadcasters (PIAC), for example, has recommended the creation of new, noncommercial educational channels to meet the educational, literacy, lifelong learning, and civic needs of underserved communities (Advisory Committee 1998, 50f.). When spectrum now used for analog broadcasting is returned to the government, according to PIAC, Congress should reserve the equivalent of 6 MHz of spectrum for each viewing community in order to realize educational and civic benefits. Focusing on the repercussions of digital television as well as broadband advanced telecommunications service delivery to the home for economic, social, and political life will be the subject of chapter 6.

Related to the development of commercially viable networks is the cost of advanced services to the home, whether they be in the form of online services, cable or satellite connections, digital broadcasting, or digital subscriber lines (Farhi 1999). Whatever the mechanisms, there are substantial costs attached to subscribing to an Internet service provider, cable television, or direct-broadcast satellite. Josh Bernoff (1998) of For-rester Research, an independent market research firm, puts the initial price of digital receivers at $4,000; price differentials between digital and analog sets will wane until the year 2004, calling into question the prospects for universal access to digital television. The consumer elec-tronics industry has been slow to develop standards for digital broadcasting, and it remains to be seen how much the set-top conversion boxes will cost consumers.

Another design element that threatens to diminish the political and civic potential of the Internet concerns the new gatekeepers, the cable operators, who view a "closed" architecture as vital to recouping their investment in the upgraded infrastructure. An open broadband network is one where customers have the ability to choose between service providers. Via one's telephone company, for example, a customer can choose any of the thousands of Internet providers now operating. A closed network forces a customer to use the bundled services offered by the cable operator, such as @Home, the principal cable-modem service provider in the country (Werbach 1999). The market imperative toward expensive pay-per-view services and the need to corral users into the net of advertisers means that citizens will be less likely to navigate noncom-mercial, civic environments online.

The concept of designing a democratic virtual public sphere impinges on the topography of cyberspace—namely, the size, shape, and location of political spaces in which persons come together to discuss issues, form opinions, or plan action. Steven Schneider (1996) calls this space "the conversational arena," the forums in which space unfolds and new conver-sations and political discussions can run their course. With respect to topography, an important issue relates to how computer-mediated com-munication (CMC) constitutes people. While many communications researchers suggest that anonymity may liberate the individual and equal-ize participation in a forum where power is otherwise asymmetrically distributed, others argue that the individual's isolation coupled with invis-ible surveillance and hierarchical observation from the outside may lead to the veritable incarceration of the user (Kiesler and Sproull 1992). A useful model developed by Russell Spears and Martin Lea (1994), called SIDE (Social Identity and Deindividuation), describes the salient identity pre-sent in CMC (e.g., personal or group identity) and its contextual features (e.g., anonymity of the in-group or identification with an in-group). Thus, the model reveals the importance of self-categorization and context dependence to a proper understanding of cognitive effects. The ramifica-tions for online political debate are important, since this model undermines any reified notions of CMC effects. As the authors argue, "there are unlikely to be universal effects of CMC because these will be determined as much by social context, the content of identities, and the nature of social relations" (1994, 452–53).

While an obvious effect of cyberspace is to break down the barriers of time and space, many recent works state this "fact" with abandon, failing to delve into its implication for politics and community. Howard Rheingold's noteworthy book *The Virtual Community* (1993) certainly popularized the discussion of electronic networks as creating virtual environments in which communities could be formed and political discussions engaged; however, Rheingold does not seriously address the epistemological and moral questions that undergird an examination of cyberspace. On the final two pages of the book, Rheingold intimates that perhaps we should remind ourselves that "electronic communication has powerful illusory capabilities" (300) and that one of the technology's entailments is that we will "forever question the reality of our online culture" (299), since we are forsaking "true" community for the virtual. However, Rheingold sidesteps the issue of what constitutes reality in a media environment. Taylor and Saarinen (1994) suggest that in the society of the spectacle, "reality is mediaized and thus becomes virtual." Thus, do not simple oppositions between the true and the apparent, the real and virtual begin to dissolve? Steven Miller also discusses the notion that "virtual communities" emerge as a result of "overcoming the obstacles of time and distance" (1996, 334), but he too does not adequately articulate what this "overcoming" entails for politics and community. He suggests that "information technology turns everything into symbolic abstractions and severs the intimacy of face-to-face connection or the feeling that actions have 'real' consequences" (336)—this in a book, not unlike Rheingold's, that signals these fundamental issues while otherwise lauding the technology for transcending time and distance.

These four characteristics of the political public sphere—antecedent resources, universal access, deliberation, and design—will now be explored in greater detail, using a multidisciplinary approach that will involve a more thorough explication of themes only intimated in this chapter. As will now be clear, the themes addressed in this book are not exhaustive, since issues such as security and privacy take a backseat to access and equity concerns. When we emerge from this journey, I will provide several remedies for salvaging democracy in the digital age from the threats caused when public-interest values remain in eclipse.

# 3

# Resource Requirements
## of Digitally Mediated Political Life

CIVIC AND POLITICAL DISCOURSE in the United States is migrating to new and powerful computer networks through which participants can share voice, video, and text (Miller 1996). The heralded town meeting has been amplified to include computer-mediated communication among and between citizens and officeholders (Guthrie and Dutton 1992; Hacker 1996). William Drake defines the emerging information infrastructure as "the computerized networks, intelligent terminals, and accompanying applications and services people use to access, create, disseminate, and utilize digital information" (1995, 5). Political candidates, parties, interest groups, and citizens with sufficient resources are now online with the realization that computer networks represent one more avenue through which they can make their voices heard and influence the policy process (Bimber 1998a, 1998b; Civille 1995; Davis 1999; R. McChesney 1997b). Resonating to this notion of a digitally enhanced public sphere, the Clinton administration's Information Infrastructure Task Force (IITF) describes this space as an "electronic commons" in which telecommunications technologies "[c]ould expand a citizen's capacity for action in local institutions" (1993, 15).

This rather idealized portrait of an electronic commons is subverted both by the resource-intensive nature of political communication and by what Herbert Schiller (1989, 1996) terms the "corporate takeover of public expression." Ownership and control of the mass media in the hands of a few corporate powers limits greatly the ability of citizens to articulate policy problems and solutions (Bagdikian 1997). As Robert McChesney puts it, "the nature of the U.S. media system undermines all three of the meaningful criteria necessary for self-government" (1997b, 7), including cultivating a sense of community and providing an effective system for political communication. One example of strictures on public speech is that as the marriage of the Internet and broadcasting becomes increasingly pay-per-use, virtual political engagement is more likely among those who can pay the cost of using computer-mediated applications (Hirschkop 1997). While I am sympathetic to this version of the economic-inequality hypothesis, which dominates the literature (Dutton, Sweet, and Rogers 1989; Murdock and Golding 1989; Golding 1997), I will argue that it is not sufficient. Resource disparities that predict the extent to which an individual will engage in online political expression must also be considered. Underscoring the primacy of economic characteristics ostensibly explains participation in digitally mediated political life by stressing a person's income; however, this link is neither as concrete nor as comprehensive as the resource approach developed hereinafter. While Peter Golding suggests that emerging electronic inequalities "reflect the underlying political economy of all previous communications technologies" (1997, 81), few specifics are given as to what mechanisms would be ameliorative, short of a massive redistribution of wealth, including the ownership of production. Nor does he discuss the noneconomic determinants of exclusion in current modes of digital communications and information exchange.

If the economic-inequality hypothesis were sufficient, for example, then public-policy solutions would need only to ensure that access to advanced telecommunications services is affordable. However, we know the picture to be more complex. In his analysis of U.S. telephone penetration, Jorge Schement (1993) found that ethnic and racial differences remain when socioeconomic status is held constant. Single-female-headed households also suffered low telephone penetration rates. An ethnographic study of one housing complex in Camden, New Jersey, revealed that mothers had reasons unrelated to income for why they did not own a telephone (Mueller and Schement 1995). The economic-inequality hypothesis ignores the fact that without antecedent resources such as literacy and what Amartya Sen (1992) terms the "capability to achieve functionings," digitally mediated political life would be unimaginable.

Sen argues that basic capabilities are of first importance in specifying citizens' needs and requirements. "Basic capabilities" refers to the overall freedom to choose between combinations of functionings, such as participating in the life of the community. Applied to basic and advanced communications technologies, the question must be asked, What basic capabilities are needed to restore citizens to their proper role as cooperating members of society? The World Institute on Disability (1994), for example, suggests that new technology has the capability of "speaking" for people with speech disabilities and "hearing" for people who are deaf, a poignant illustration of the sort of argument that is made for ubiquitous access to these tools. Thomas Jefferson intimates a resource model in his famous letter to Edward Carrington in which the statesman proclaimed that if he had to decide whether to have a government without newspapers or newspapers without government, he would prefer the latter. After Jefferson made this remarkable statement, he qualified it in the very next sentence by saying, "I should mean that every man should receive those papers & be capable of reading them" ([1787] 1984, 880). In other words, Jefferson knew that ubiquitous dissemination of affordable media is necessary, but people must have the capability to use these media to exercise substantive freedoms (Garnham 1990; Streck 1998).

I suggest in this chapter that attention to background or antecedent conditions translates into the ability to take part in the life of the community by concentrating on the distribution of essential resources as well as the conversion of these resources into freedoms. By some accounts, one of these freedoms is access to telecommunications (Pool 1983); however, without the concomitant capacity to act, this freedom cannot be successfully exercised. While the Telecommunications Act of 1996 was predicated on the availability of services "at just, reasonable, and affordable rates," other resource requirements for salutary involvement in the life of the community (via electronic media) have consistently been ignored. This chapter suggests that serious attention needs to be paid not only to how affordable rates are (although this is essential), but also to a person's antecedent resources and capacities in order to achieve the goals of a more universally accessible and participatory public sphere in cyberspace, one that takes us well beyond the enervated prescriptions of recent telecommunications legislation.

## Toward a Resource Model of Telecommunications Access

The model I am proffering to explain access to and use of emerging communications networks for political purposes is a *resource model of technology access*. At the broad conceptual level, the resource model both clarifies the connecting links and provides causal inferences that explain the relationship between a person's capacity and her participation in digitally mediated political discourse. The acquisition, possession, and utilization of resources are usually implied rather than fully explicated in models of technology access and use that fasten to socioeconomic deter-

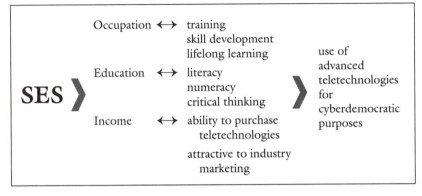

Figure 3.1 A Resource Model of Digitally Mediated Political Life

minants. These resources are like stepping-stones, connecting one's socioeconomic status to the achievement of certain functionings (i.e., participation in the life of the community).

This model is stronger in three ways than existing models that fail either to go beyond asymmetrical economic relations in explaining technology access (Murdock and Golding 1989; Dutton, Sweet, and Rogers 1989; Golding 1997) or to specify the mechanisms that link socioeconomic status to computer-mediated engagement (Anderson et al. 1995; Civille 1995; McConnaughey 1997). First, it is more analytically rigorous. That is to say, an attempt is made to link socioeconomic status to participation in the virtual public sphere via an analysis of one's capacities and resources. As Sen suggests, "economic means cannot be judged independently of the actual possibilities of 'converting' incomes and resources into capability to function" (1992, 110). Second, it is more comprehensive than traditional models that reduce technology gaps to socioeconomic status. A model that solely addresses socioeconomic status, for example, does not adequately explain ethnic, racial, and gender differences in computer ownership, as will be shown.

Finally, the resource model allows one to make causal inferences about how certain connecting links explain the relationship between skills, socioeconomic status, and participation in digitally mediated political life. In other words, the resources one brings to bear on potential political participation in cyberspace can be traced back to the acquisition of skills and the cultivation of knowledge and experience in the family, at school, and on the job. Such an explanation establishes a causal relation, as figure 3.1 illustrates, between institutional involvement and political activity. Rather than saying that educational attainment explains advanced telecommunications access and use, perhaps the analytical link needs to be made that background conditions such as the acquisition of literacy, technology experience, and a readiness to learn create an environment in which online political involvement becomes a more likely possibility for underprivileged and undertrained persons (U.S. Department of Education 1997). Thus inferences are made unpacking the precise mechanisms by which the cultivation of resources affects online political involvement.

Let me illustrate the sorts of resources and capacities involved in digitally mediated political life to suggest ways in which the model sheds light on necessary antecedent conditions for participation in the virtual public sphere. This model is similar in many ways to Verba, Schlozman, and Brady's (1995) "civic voluntarism model" in which resources, engagement, and recruitment explain political activity. Critical resources include what the authors describe as civic skills, such as writing letters, giving speeches, and organizing meetings. The ability to communicate, for example, is a fundamental human skill that presupposes, among other things, linguistic facility and cultural familiarity. At the individual level, socialization patterns, educational goals, and interactive capabilities intertwine to allow the individual to participate in everyday speech, understanding, and action (Habermas 1987). Similar conditions are undoubtedly at work in online political engagement, wherein participants require a modicum of literacy, training, facility with the technology, and a feeling of self-efficacy that would motivate citizens to participate in the first place. While neo-Marxist authors are correct in underscoring the primacy of economics in explaining who will own important communications sluices in a market-driven society, they paint with broad brush strokes, discounting the antecedent (noneconomic) conditions necessary to achieve functioning. The hypothesis to be tested can be expressed as follows: resources and capacities are the precise mechanisms—intervening between socioeconomic status and online political activity—that appropriately address causality while also providing a comprehensive, analytically sound model for explaining access to digitally mediated political life.

## Data

This study relies principally on Current Population Survey (CPS) data from the November 1994 and December 1998 Computer Ownership/Internet Supplements. The Bureau of the Census conducts the CPS monthly and is the source of data published by the Bureau of Labor Statistics. In October

1984, 1989, 1993, and 1997 as well as November 1994 and December 1998 the CPS added supplements on computer access and use. About 56,100 occupied housing units were eligible for interviews, and there were approximately 157,000 observations in the sample for the November 1994 survey. The December 1998 survey included 48,000 household interviews. This latter survey is available through Ferret, a tool developed and supported by the U.S. Bureau of the Census to extract data from these surveys. Ferret allows one to ascertain frequencies and cross tabulations for variables but does not support advanced statistical manipulations of data. Thus the November 1994 data set was used to test hypotheses related to the resource model of digitally mediated political life, while the more recent December 1998 data were used to present the most current descriptive data on computer ownership and e-mail and Internet use. The unit of analysis applicable to CPS data can be ascribed either to the household or to the individual. This analysis uses the household as the appropriate unit of analysis.

The predictor variables that serve as the basis of the logistic regression analysis are family income, educational attainment, occupational status, gender, race, and ethnicity. Income is a continuous variable, measured in thousands of dollars, representing the combined income of all family members. Educational attainment is also continuous, defined as the highest level of school completed or degree received by the respondent. Occupational status is broken down by major occupational categories, including managerial and professional (knowledge workers), service, production, and agriculture. Race is a categorical variable defined as White, Black, Asian or Pacific Islander, American Indian, Aleut or Eskimo, and other. Ethnicity is a dichotomous variable, defined as being Hispanic or non-Hispanic. These variables will be explained further in the context of the findings below. The dichotomous dependent variables are: whether there is a computer in a household, whether the householder uses e-mail and the Internet, and whether that computer is being used to engage in political activity. The last of these is a composite of three variables that together provide an approximation or proxy of what characterizes digitally mediated political life. These variables are: whether the household computer is used to communicate with friends, family, and others; whether the computer is used to access government information; and whether the householder would be interested in using the computer to vote from home.

## Methods

Logistic regression analysis was chosen as the appropriate statistical tool, since it regresses a dichotomous dependent variable on a set of independent variables. This technique allows estimations of the probability that events will occur, with the logistic coefficient interpreted as the change in the log-odds associated with a one-unit change in the independent variable. Since log-odds are difficult to interpret, they can be translated into odds by using the formula 1 divided by 1 plus $e$ (the base for Naperian, or natural, logarithms, equal to about 2.72) raised to the power of the (negative) coefficient, $B$. Hence: Prob [event]/Prob [no event] = $1/1+e^{-z}$. If one is dealing with categorical data rather than continuous independent variables, then the interpretation of the odds of accessing a computer with a change in a category is different. For example, the variable JOB is divided into four categories, only three of which actually appear in the table. If we examine JOB(1) in Appendix A1 (those individuals who are managers or professionals), the Exp($B$)=1.4392. In other words, the odds increase by a factor of 1.44 that professionals will own a home computer compared to all occupational categories.

## "Thick Description" of Teletechnology Access and Use

Appendices A1–A3 provide clear and compelling portraits of the relationship between online (political) engagement and a host of independent variables. What strikes the eye is that educational attainment, along with family income, are stronger predictors of computer ownership and online use. The primacy of educational attainment—and the skills, training, and literacy that accompany educational success—brings into relief the importance of resources to full participation in digital democracy. Income and occupation are also central to any understanding of what it takes to be at the center of the information society. In addition, as the logistic regression analysis shows, differences in teletechnology access and use by race, ethnicity, and gender are not adequately explained by traditional socioeconomic indicators, which suggests that there are noneconomic reasons why in general Blacks, Hispanics, and women remain more or less on the periphery of social, civic, and political life in cyberspace.

Analyzing the Current Population Survey data reveals a strong correlation between household income and computer ownership, modem access, and network use. Eighteen percent of households with income under $25,000 had a computer in December 1998, compared to 43 percent of households earning between $25,000 and $50,000 and 73 percent of those households with income over $50,000. Analysis of

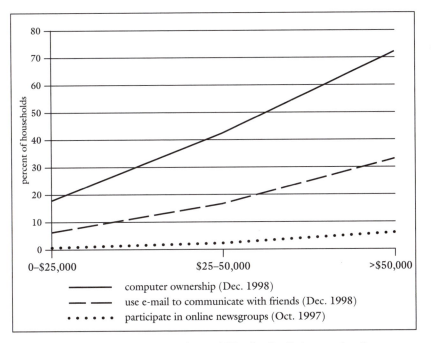

Figure 3.2 Teletechnology Ownership and Use (by family income level)
(*Source:* U.S. Department of the Census, Current Population Survey, December 1998,
October 1997)

home Internet use reveals a similar dynamic, with only 8 percent of
low-income households using the Internet in 1998, compared to 21
percent of middle-income individuals and 44 percent of households
with incomes at or above $50,000. In terms of income level and online
social, civic, and political engagement, there is also a positive relationship. As figure 3.2 shows, only about 6 percent of households with
incomes below $25,000 use their computer to send and receive e-mail
and to communicate with others, while 34 percent of households with
incomes above $50,000 are using computers to communicate with the
outside world. Participation in newsgroups, moreover, is extremely rare
in households with incomes under the $25,000 mark, 1 percent. The
figure for households with incomes above $50,000 is only 6 percent,
which suggests that online political engagement—in particular, the use
of newsgroups to shape policy issues—remains an extremely exclusive
activity.

Along with the earning power of the family, educational attainment is
fundamental in understanding the extent to which one can participate in

digitally mediated political communication. Of those households access-ing the Internet in December 1998, 81 percent had attended some college. Among those who had attained less than a tenth-grade educa-tion, only 9 percent of households had a home computer in 1998. The figure was 31 percent household penetration for those with a high-school degree, a percentage that more than doubles, to 67 percent, for those with a bachelor's degree. While gains were significant for all groups between 1994 and 1998, the huge (and growing) gaps in teletechnology ownership by educational attainment are striking.

In terms of using e-mail to communicate with friends, one percent of householders with below a tenth-grade education were using e-mail from home, compared to 9 percent with a high-school degree and 34 percent of (four-year) college graduates. Finally, the tally for home Internet use was 2 percent of householders with less than ten years of formal school-ing, 12 percent for high-school graduates, and 42 percent for those with bachelor's degrees. As is clear from the data, the overwhelming majority of households using the Internet are highly educated. Indeed, education is a stronger determinant of connectivity than is any other variable. Figure 3.3 shows that education correlates highly with the use of computer net-works to communicate and participate in newsgroups. Fewer than 1 percent of householders with less than a tenth-grade education are using computers to send and receive e-mail compared with over one-third of those with a college degree. In terms of participation in newsgroups, including political newsgroups, approximately one household in six hun-dred with less than a tenth-grade education is active in online newsgroups, while 6 percent of college graduates are subscribing to these newsgroups.

Not surprisingly, those persons who occupy "knowledge work" posi-tions—such as professionals and managers—are more likely to use a computer on the job than workers in service, agriculture, or manufactur-ing. As of December 1998, 71 percent of all employed persons who use a home computer are knowledge workers, and the figures are even higher for e-mail (79 percent) and home Internet use (78 percent). These pro-portions are relatively unchanged since 1994, which suggests that computers remain the domain of knowledge workers, the elite managers and professionals of the global information society (Aurigi and Graham 1998; Castells 1998). According to the December 1998 CPS, moreover, 62 percent of managers and professionals owned a home computer, com-pared to 37 percent of production and agriculture workers. Of managers, professionals, technicians, and sales workers, 37 percent used the Internet from home, compared to 12 percent of agricultural workers and 15 per-

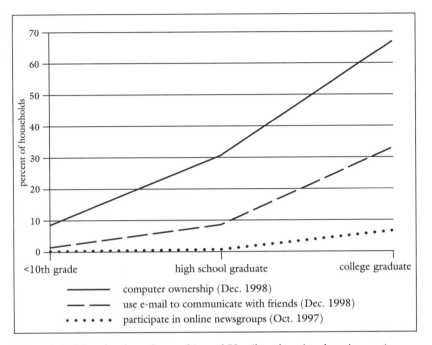

Figure 3.3 Teletechnology Ownership and Use (by educational attainment)
(*Source:* U.S. Department of the Census, Current Population Survey, December 1998, October 1997)

cent of production workers. The logistic regression analyses shown in appendices A1 and A2 show that one's occupation is a statistically significant variable that explains computer ownership and network use, even when income and educational attainment are held constant, at least for managers and professionals.

Hispanics and African Americans lag behind Whites in home computer access and network use. According to the U.S. Department of Commerce's *Falling through the Net* report:

> The "digital divide" is now one of America's leading economic and civil rights issues. This year's report finds that a digital divide still exists, and, in many cases, is actually *widening* over time.
> (U. S. Department of Commerce 1999, xiii)

While the computer ownership figure for non-Hispanic White households was about 47 percent in late 1998, the figure was a dismal 26 percent for Hispanic and 23 percent for African-American households. The gap in computer ownership grew significantly between 1994 and 1998. When it comes to being connected, the data are even more troubling. Twenty-two percent of White households are using e-mail from home, while only 8 percent of Hispanic and African-American households are e-mailing friends and family. Finally, approximately 9 percent of Hispanic and African-American households use the Internet at home, compared to 27 percent of non-Hispanic White huseholds. The logistic regression analysis suggests that race and ethnicity predict computer ownership independently of other socioeconomic indicators (appendix A1). Thus, those who say that Hispanics or African Americans do not own computers in large numbers due to their disproportionately high poverty levels tell only part of the story (Walsh 1999).

In terms of differences between men and women in access to and use of computers and the Internet, recent data show that there are substantial differences in computer ownership, e-mail access, and Internet use by gender, with thirteen, six, and four percentage-point differences, respectively. Of householders who use the Internet from home, for example, 67 percent are men, suggesting a gender gap in Internet use that cannot be explained by controlling for socioeconomic characteristics. Of male householders in the United States, moreover, 26 percent were online in late 1998, while the figure for females was 17 percent, a significant difference. Just as with race and ethnicity, differences in computer, modem, and network access and use between men and women are not explained sufficiently by socioeconomic determinants.

## Noneconomic Barriers

The foregoing overview of the findings provides ample evidence for the resource model of technology access. Disparities in computer ownership and Internet use as well as in the use of these tools to engage in social, civic, and political discussion are strongly associated with various background factors, such as race, ethnicity, gender, educational attainment, and employment level. While differences in access to and use of advanced communications technologies among minority groups are confounded by gaps in the average socioeconomic level between minority and non-Hispanic White families, significant differences persist when socioeconomic status is held constant. The data lend support (1) for an analytically rigorous and comprehensive link explaining the relationship among (a) resources, (b) race, ethnicity, and gender, and (c) access to and use of advanced telecommunications tools, and (2) for a clear causal connection between antecedent resource development and engagement in online social, civic, and political activity.

## Why Resources Matter: A Closer Look
## at Race, Ethnicity, and Gender

While a person's socioeconomic status—including income, educational attainment, and occupational status—goes a long way in explaining access to and use of capital- and knowledge-intensive information and communications technologies, an analysis of race, ethnicity, and gender supports the notion that a better theoretical link is needed relating these attributes to technology access. The resource model suggests that social context and cultural norms acquired during the course of one's involvement with familial, occupational, educational, and social institutions explain why certain individuals in society lag behind others even when we account for their socioeconomic situation.

Let us start with gender. The hypothesis developed here is that cultural norms and social contexts play a role in explaining the differential rate of home computer penetration. The notion of "separate cultures" of younger boys and girls can be extended to explain the gender bias that seems to surround the promotion of computers in society in general and schools and universities in particular. As Milton Chen (1986) suggests, "the development of skill with computers is more socially approved and offers more social incentives in the culture of adolescent males than females" (279). Study after study in the fields of education, psychology, and communications have found that significant differences persist between male and female children, adolescents, and college students. Male students interested in computers have more role models (Cottrell 1992); they are more strongly encouraged to pursue computer-related career paths (Spertus 1991); and even the design of "netiquette rules," according to some researchers, present a bias toward male discursive norms over those of females (Herring 1994). Hess and Miura (1985) discovered that across all age groups through high school, three times as many boys as girls attended computer camps, and this gap increased with grade, cost of program, and level of difficulty of course offered. When attitudes were sampled in the context of the perceived value of computers for future employment, Gardner, McEwen, and Curry (1986) found that high-school boys expressed at a significantly higher rate than girls the belief that computers would be important in determining their employment prospects. A three-year study by Krendl, Brohier, and Fleetwood found, moreover, that "despite the significant influence of computer use, the pattern of results for differential sex effects favoring boys remained" (1989, 91). In short, if women are not encouraged to follow career paths in which computers play a central role, they will not develop the skills, resources, talents, and interest to become full participants in digitally mediated political life.

This explanation suggests that as the computer culture changes to include greater input from women, we should expect the gender gap to abate. Sherry Turkle, for example, calls computerphobia a "transitional phenomenon" (1988, 41), an artifact of the early days of the computer revolution in which its language and feel were embedded in rigid and formal environments, antithetical to the way in which women experience and orient themselves in the world. Turkle's hopeful vision is that once computers are taught and introduced as a flexible and expressive medium and environment, then women will establish more of a personal relationship with the computer:

> When people are put in computer-rich environments, supported by flexible and powerful programming languages, and encouraged to use the computer as an expressive material, they respond in a diversity of styles . . . unlike stereotypes of a machine with which there is only one way of relating, the computer can be a partner in a great diversity of relationships. (1988, 57)

Turkle's sanguine outlook regarding the long-term use of computers by women is supported by social science research being conducted at Carnegie Mellon University. Fisher, Margolis, and Miller (1997) find that what prevents young women from pursuing computer science professions are "cultural artifacts" that stand in their way, including women's perceptions of these fields as well as the institutional culture within the nation's top research departments. These, of course, can be changed, but it may take some time before the climate of these institutions and the attitudes women have about computer science and related professions are transformed.

Examining longitudinal CPS data from 1984 to 1998 reveals a growing gap in home computer ownership (see figure 3.4) between non-Hispanic Whites and ethnic and racial minorities. While rapid changes in technology have created opportunity for some in U.S. society, others who lack the skills and resources to be more fully integrated in economic, social, and political life have been pushed to the margins. The hypothesis put forth is that given lower levels of access to and use of advanced telecommunications tools at work and in the home among Hispanic and African-American families, a critical mass has yet to be achieved in these communities that would establish a cultural norm or an acceptance level of the technologies. Since accreditation of the value of computer technology

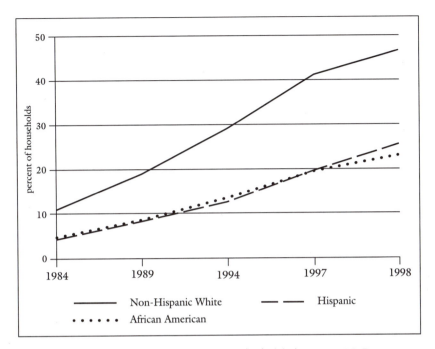

Figure 3.4 Computer Ownership (by race and ethnicity) (*Source:* U.S. Department of the Census, Current Population Survey, December 1998, November 1994, October 1984, 1989, 1997)

is at least partially a function of one's experience with and exposure to the technology, the relative lack of family members, neighbors, and work associates who can vouch for the worth of computers and their application to politics may very well translate into lower ownership and use levels among ethnic and racial minorities (Rogers and Kincaid 1981).

This quasi-sociological perspective has been articulated by a growing body of scholars and journalists who see great attitudinal and perceptual barriers separating ethnic and racial minorities from the mainstream of American society. Anthony Walton (1999) suggests, for example, that certain technologies have in many ways made things worse for African Americans, since Blacks have failed in many instances to do the things necessary to reap the rewards of technological progress: "not channeled to follow the largely technological possibilities for success in this society, black folkways have instead embraced the sort of magical thinking that is encouraged by the media and corporations whose sole interest in blacks is as consumers" (18). I would take issue with this statement only to suggest that some in the high-tech and telecommunications industries will take no interest in Blacks, even as consumers, if they are perceived to be an unprofitable market (Wilhelm 1998b).

Among Hispanic adults in the United States, a large portion remains disconnected from the information superhighway discourse that has circulated throughout most of society in the late 1990s. As of early 1998, for example, almost one-third of all Hispanics had never used a computer, and a larger segment of the adult population responded that it had no use either for computers or the Internet (Wilhelm 1998a; U. S. Department of Commerce 1999). The culture of computing and online activity therefore has yet to find value among those who have little experience with and exposure to these information and communications technologies. Another setback for Hispanics is linguistic. Since the Internet remains a largely English-dominant medium, what is to be done for the one-quarter of Hispanic adults who would prefer to access the Internet in Spanish?

Lingering social perceptions about the appropriate career paths and role of women in society as well as notions of the ability of minority communities to participate in the virtual public sphere lend support to the resource model described in this chapter. If women are discouraged from developing computer literacy and pursuing career paths in which computer facility is part and parcel of doing the job, then they will not develop important resources at the same rate as others, such as computer literacy and lifelong-learning skills. If minorities are perceived as marginalized actors in the dominant society's euphoria over information technology, then they too will not see the value in cultivating certain skills and training. To the extent that these barriers remain, the growing technology gap may continue to widen and the skills needed to succeed will be passed on within certain groups that already participate in the center of economic and political life, while those on the periphery (not only women and ethnic and racial minorities but also people with disabilities, inhabitants of rural areas, and the elderly) will remain outside of the mainstream.

### The Internet Does Not Look like America

Certain academics (Birdsell et al. 1998) and pollsters (Pew Research Center 1999) spread the good news that the Internet has begun to resemble America in all of its diversity. In its January 1999 survey gauging Internet use in the United States, the Pew Research Center pointed out that the Internet audience is "getting decidedly mainstream," resembling a broader cross section of the American public. Today one cannot escape the soothsayers of the virtual life who read into the information and com-

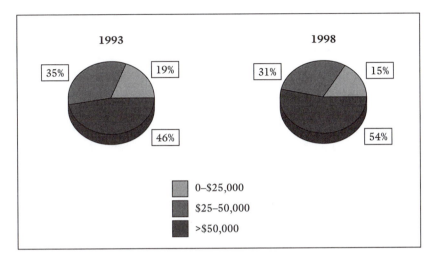

Figure 3.5 Computer-Owning Households (1993 v. 1998) (by family income)
(*Source:* U.S. Department of the Census, Current Population Survey, December 1998,
October 1993)

munications revolutions signs of a more salutary social order to come.
The print and electronic media pinpoint new haunts on the Internet
where netizens can engage in commerce, recreation, and information
seeking. Such activities bode well for the segment of society in the digital
age who can purchase and use these tools in the comfort of their own
homes, while a significant underclass may remain disconnected or relegated to infrequent use at the city library or nearby community center.

Telecommunications company spokespeople argue that the Internet is
becoming mainstream to justify greater deregulation of the industry, suggesting that the information revolution remains on the right track as long
as the (invisible) hands of the market are further unbound. Some academics and pollsters, moreover, have taken a look at changes in computer
and Internet ownership demographics and have equated increased penetration rates with expanded diversity of ownership. Such an analysis
misses the mark.

As figure 3.5 shows, between 1993 and 1998 computer ownership,
rather than trickling down to the lower and middle strata of society, has
actually become slightly more concentrated in affluent segments of society. For example, in 1993, of all computer-owning households, 19
percent had an annual family income below $25,000. Five years later, the
figure was down to 15 percent, suggesting that computer ownership has
hitherto accreted in the stratum of well-to-do households rather than rar-
ifying throughout American domiciles.

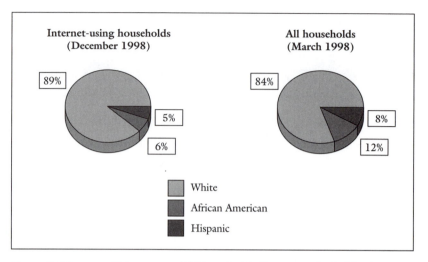

Figure 3.6 Internet-Using versus All Households (by race and ethnicity )
(*Source:* U.S. Department of the Census, Current Population Survey, December 1998, October 1997)

Another way of getting at this issue is to compare household Internet use to the racial and ethnic breakdown by domicile for the nation as a whole. As figure 3.6 illustrates, the Internet continues to represent disproportionately non-Hispanic White users while Blacks and Hispanics are severely "underrepresented." For example, although 12 percent of all households in the United States are Black, only 6 percent of Internet-using households are Black, a contrast that undermines the oversanguine view that the distribution of information and communications technologies is beginning to look like America along important socioeconomic, racial, and ethnic lines.

The misconceptions about computer-owning and Internet-subscribing households resembling the diversity of American society underwrites an agenda that equates technological development with progress. To believe that the elitism of the information society will give way to an egalitarian social order legitimizes the information age in the eyes of those who benefit most. Advertising slogans such as Microsoft's blithe question "Where do you want to go today?" promises that computer networks can take people places they have never been. However, the two characteristics endorsed in this message—mobility and direction—are lost on persons who may be semiliterate, language-limited, or apprehensive about navigating an unfamiliar technology environment. MCI WorldCom proclaims, moreover, that the "World is officially open for business," although most of the planet's population has yet to make a telephone call, let alone engage in e-business.

## The Causal Priority of Family and Education

In clarifying the relative importance of antecedent resources, the causal priority of institutions such as the family and schools is brought into relief, as illustrated by figure 3.1. According to the Third International Mathematics and Science Study (TIMSS), parental involvement and the presence of educational resources in the home, including the presence of a computer, are strong predictors of academic development in math and science among fourth- and eighth-graders (Third International Mathematics and Science Study 1997). The U.S. Department of Education's report *The Social Context of Education*, moreover, suggests that parents' education, family structure, and the environment in which students learn were particularly salient in predicting educational success (U.S. Department of Education 1997). As John Dewey ([1916] 1966) underscored, education is a process of "preparation or getting ready" to participate in and adapt to the challenges of adult life. Dewey's organic metaphor of education as growth, process, and unfolding underscores the value of cultivating and nourishing certain capacities in people from the outset, capacities that will provide a toehold in a changing, technology-intensive society.

In addition to fostering a readiness to learn and critical thinking in the home and in educational institutions, the cultivation of lifelong learning at work may help prepare individuals to engage in an information society. As Peter Drucker (1993) suggests, "universal literacy of a very high order is the first priority . . . without it, no society can hope to be capable of high performance" (198). As the data show, those persons whose knowledge base and skills are becoming obsolescent, such as those employed in manufacturing or agriculture, may not have the capacity to retool, since they have hitherto lacked the skills that afford a competitive advantage in knowledge-related work. As Robert Reich underscores, "people fortunate enough to have had an excellent education followed by on-the-job experience doing complex things can become steadily more valuable over time, making it difficult for others ever to catch up" (1991, 109). Recent trends point to the upgrading of the occupational structure as postindustrial society requires workers who are more highly skilled. Simultaneously, occupational polarization increases as the top and the bottom of the social ladder grow farther apart.

Due to resource disparities, those who are already disadvantaged struggle to keep pace in economic (Economic Policy Institute 1999), social (Castells 1998), and political life (Bimber 1998a, 1998b). Technology gaps will very likely exacerbate these inequalities, which means that low-income and minority individuals will run faster only to remain on the periphery of society. The causal priority of education, parent involvement, lifelong learning, social context, and literacy suggest ways in which inequalities can be mitigated, solutions that may be easier to put down on paper than to implement in an environment hostile to large-scale policy initiatives, particularly those that fetter the marketplace.

# 4

# Immune to Progress:
# Reconceptualizing America's Information
# and Telecommunications Underclass

IN HIS PRESCIENT BOOK *The Other America*, Michael Harrington examined the underbelly of the affluent society, exposing the extravagance of its claim to have solved the grinding economic problems of the age related to basic human needs. Harrington's sobering retort to the optimism of the affluent society was to describe its negative analogue—what he called "the other America"—in which one-third of Americans were mired in poverty. Describing this underclass as "immune to progress" (1962, 13), Harrington suggested that as the economy becomes more technology-reliant, the ranks of the poor expand, since "good jobs require much more academic preparation, much more skill from the very outset." Today, almost two generations later, the information society—an extension of what Marx and Engels called "the world market" ([1848] 1978, 475)—claims to raise the standard of living of most, while many detractors have spotted the new other America in the midst of superabundance (Friedman 1999). Secluded and marginalized from progress, these have-nots embody many of the same characteristics of 1950s-style poverty, while also lacking access to advanced information and telecommunications services. This exclusion from the means to participate in the virtual public sphere shatters the idols of those who see in advanced television and telecommunications services, as currently arranged and deployed, the key to perpetuating American-style democracy well into the twenty-first century.

This chapter aims to refine the current notion of an information underclass by describing exactly who remains immune to progress in what Wilson Carey McWilliams (1993) calls "the technological republic." In describing the information and telecommunications poor, I will defend a new taxonomy of teletechnology poverty that goes beyond the Manichean have/have-not distinction suffusing the current literature. An analysis of a segmented underclass is undertaken, one that disaggregates existing information poverty. A more appropriate subdivision of information poverty can assist policy makers to craft universal-service programs that meet the diverse information and communications needs of a sprawling underclass rather than molding a monolithic policy. The first part of this chapter highlights the difficulties that must be surmounted to identify and define clearly what amounts to a moving target, information and telecommunications poverty. Next, I will defend an expanded definition of information poverty, a periphery-center model that differentiates five divisions of have-nots. This theoretical scheme will be supported by empirical data from a national survey of Hispanic adults, called the Hispanic Computer and Internet Study (HCIS), a random-sample survey of advanced telecommunications technology and computer ownership and use patterns. Finally, I will profile each of the categories of information poverty, including those who are immune to progress, to suggest that progress in a new society must include a measurement of how technological advancement impacts the underprivileged. Actualizing this principle will take concerted social and political action, a subject to which I shall return in chapter 7 and the conclusion.

## A Tale of Two Cities

The subtext of the Clinton administration's otherwise euphoric vision of a widespread information infrastructure is a Dickensian tale about two cities: one in which the best of times prevails among those who can benefit from advanced telecommunications services, and another experiencing the worst of times due to information and technology poverty. The information underclass has been part and parcel of the National Information Infrastructure (NII) discourse since its inception. The 1993 *Agenda for Action* underscored that "as a matter of fundamental fairness, this nation cannot accept a division of our people among telecommunication or information 'haves' and 'have nots'" (Information Infrastructure Task Force 1993, 8), and this sentiment has been echoed throughout the Clinton administration's tenure in defense of its NII initiatives. For example, the new universal-service fund aimed at providing discounted telecommunications services for schools and libraries in poor and rural communities (§254 of the Telecommunications Reform Act of 1996) has come under fire from certain telecommunications companies, U.S. senators, and consumer advocates, an affront deflected by Vice President Gore, who argued that "we must bridge the digital divide between the information haves and have nots to ensure that all Americans can take advantage of the Internet" (White House press release, April 22, 1998).

While political considerations might warrant portraying information poverty in overly simplistic terms, one would expect policy research and other scholarship on the subject to refine and clarify rather than reify these distinctions. However, much of the recent work on the subject of information and telecommunications inequality has accepted this binary distinction between haves and have-nots. Richard Civille suggests, for example, that the growth of the public Internet may signal "the emergence of a two-tiered society of information haves and have nots" (1995, 175), particularly since ownership and use of advanced teletechnologies have soared disproportionately among highly educated and more affluent individuals. V.J.J.M. Bekkers shares Civille's anxiety in his description of "a new division in society: the information 'haves' and 'have nots'" (1997, 164). This access gap, according to Bekkers, is caused by reliance on the personal computer as the gateway to the Internet, a market force privileging mainly highly educated, young, and male network users. In their study of Internet use among African Americans in the United States, Donna Hoffman and Thomas Novak explore the consequences of "a 'digital divide' between the information 'haves' and 'have nots'" (1998, 390), one where income and education largely drive the inequalities present between racial groups. Raab and colleagues articulate a concern about the need to alleviate the gap in access to information, so critical in supporting democratic values, a chasm that the authors presume takes the form of a two-tiered distinction (1996, 285). Finally, James McConnaughey (1997), a senior economist with the National Telecommunications and Information Administration, provides an administration perspective, consonant with its 1999 *Falling through the Net* report, in which telecommunications have-nots are identified by their socioeconomic status, race, and geography.

What is clear from these policy analyses and academic works is that the signifier *have-not* is appropriated to represent a monolithic and static information and telecommunications underclass, often without an attempt at distinguishing conceptually or theoretically varying degrees of marginality. This term serves primarily as a placeholder in situations where a have-not lacks access to a platform of putatively essential information services (emergency, medical, or employment) or the latest technology (a telephone, a digital subscriber line, or the provision of Internet service). Used in the academic press, the term is usually unpacked and explained by referring exclusively to a person's demographic profile (and, in all fairness, this is usually all the data allow). What remains missing from this analysis is a broader context of a person's information-seeking behavior, media use patterns, and cultural and environmental contexts, features providing a thicker description of the various shades of information and telecommunications inequalities (Schön, Sanyal, and Mitchell 1999).

Of course, not all of the literature is mired in these dualistic distinctions. The recent edited volume *Cyberspace Divide* takes a close look at this issue, and many of its authors take on this issue with considerable nuance. Brian Loader's introductory chapter sets the tone for this excellent investigation: "the 'information-poor' are no more an homogeneous social phenomenon then their wealthier counterparts. Fragmented and divided by gender, race, disability, class, location or religion, their experience of ICTs [information and communications technology] will vary enormously as will their opportunities to utilise it" (1998, 9). This chapter proceeds in the spirit of exploring and uncovering more precisely various layers of information poverty, including the attitudes and perceptions shared by the poor toward the information society.

Before defending an alternative model to the dichotomous have/have-not distinction that dominates the literature, it is necessary to describe the difficulties of conceptualizing information and telecommunications poverty. There are at least four dilemmas in conceptualizing and subdividing an information underclass. Addressing directly these problems contributes to a clearer understanding of the slipperiness of the concepts under investigation and directs us toward their more refined conceptualization.

First, the technology or medium that modifies the term *have-not* is subject to alteration as creative destruction occurs in the marketplace. Joseph Schumpeter ([1942] 1975) coined the term *creative destruction* to refer to the rapid economic and technological transformations that typify societies dominated by market economies (Wilhelm 1996). His analysis borrowed heavily from the *Communist Manifesto*—in particular, Marx and Engels's contention that under the capitalist mode of production "all that is solid melts into air" ([1848] 1978, 476). The meaning of this seemingly whimsical phrase is that what Marx and Engels derisively refer to as "free competition" unleashes productive forces, an ineluctable consequence being the "uninterrupted disturbance of all social conditions, everlasting uncertainty and agitation." With telecommunications and media products and services transforming themselves every six to eighteen months and with financial markets teetering, the "disturbances" levied on the subaltern are clear (Castells 1998; Soros 1998). As Murdock and Golding define the dilemma, "by their very nature, these goods [i.e., video and home computers] cumulatively advantage their owners and provide access to expensive and extensive value-added facilities, so that poorer groups are chasing a moving and fast-receding target" (1989, 192). As a result of creative destruction, coupled with the inability or unwillingness of policy

makers to keep up with market flux, the poor become stratified or segmented, existing at various levels of technological capacity (Walton 1999;
Rifkin 1995, chap. 5). Taking into account this stratification is imperative
to understand what drives differential telecommunications poverty in
America. The Telecommunications Act of 1996, §254(c)(1), provides a
dynamic definition of universal service: "an evolving level of telecommunications services." However, policy makers at the FCC have yet to
reconcile new universal-service mechanisms with the procompetitive,
deregulated environment it has conjured in the wake of the act.

The second complexity of defining have-nots—and a corollary to the
first problem—relates to the elision (due to media convergence) of the
difference between telecommunications tools as transportation or transmission media and as content carriers (Lenert 1998). The media
convergence under way requires a broadening of the conception of
telecommunications poverty to include content concerns. As Williams
and Hadden suggest, "the availability of new technologies . . . forces us
to consider *content*, an element not included in the traditional definition
of universal service for voice telephone" (1992, 403). After the passage
of the 1996 Telecommunications Act, moreover, the local exchange carriers can become vertically integrated, full-service providers of data
transmission and content, once viable competition in the local market has
been established. Such a state of affairs leads to the further erosion of the
separate spheres of content and transport.

If we assume that there is a lack of information among the less well-to-
do, then must we not discover what their information needs are before
deploying new services (Dutton 1994)? This process of defining a diversity
of community needs—and, concomitantly, permitting the public to voice
its concerns and to produce content (see Downmunt 1993)—is precisely
what many telecommunications and broadcast companies have abandoned
over the past twenty years (Dahlgren 1998; Lloyd 1997; Krasnow 1997).
In testimony before the Advisory Committee on Public Interest Obligations of Digital Television Broadcasters (PIAC), for example, Andrew
Schwartzman argues that the public interest should include "discussion of
local issues, sharing publicly owned spectrum with members of the public,
meeting the needs of children, the disabled, and of those who are too old,
too poor, too young to be demographically attractive" (Schwartzman
1997, 54). This sentiment was embodied in the final PIAC report as a concern for localism, including airing local services as they are ascertained by
public-service media and other noncommercial organizations, not just by
broadcasters (Advisory Committee 1998, 27 ff.). Any conceptualization of
information poverty should include as a point of departure, among other

things, the diverse needs of local communities as residents define them, not as conceived by information brokers.

The third caveat concerning the definition of information and technology poverty concerns where advanced service should be deployed. With the passage of the 1996 Telecommunications Act, universal service in the United States has been amended to include institutions hitherto excluded from consideration, such as libraries, schools, and rural health care providers (Blau 1997). This new policy has its critics, since it is unclear whether wiring public-access locations will provide sufficient assistance for low-income users when many if not most of their more affluent cohorts have home Internet access. As Robert McChesney asserts, "schools and libraries are often pointed to as the key agents that will democratize computer usage, yet these institutions are in the throes of long-term cut-backs that seem to render absurd the notion that they could undertake this mission" (1996, 114). Underlying McChesney's reservations regarding the ameliorative effects of the Snowe-Rockefeller provision of the 1996 Telecommunications Act is a concern about where (and, by implication, to whom) advanced telecommunications should be deployed to provide truly universal access for the information underclass. By many accounts, wiring schools and libraries is neither a necessary nor a sufficient condition for quality, universal access to advanced services (as implied by §706 of the Telecommunications Act). If locating Internet stations in libraries is taken to be sufficient to meet the needs of low-income and minority residents, then we might be unwittingly reifying the accessibility gap. I will return to this issue in chapter 6 with a more thorough analysis of the debate over home-based versus public-access deployment of advanced telecommunications services.

Finally, the fourth difficulty with existing categorizations (as was addressed in the previous chapter) concerns the extent to which antecedent resource and skill development are included in a definition of information poverty. Without the acquisition of literacy, resources, and information-seeking skills, advanced information and communications technologies are for all intents and purposes unusable (Loader 1998). As Schement and Curtis suggest, "computer literacy requires knowledge of traditional literacy as much as the oral-visual proficiencies envisioned by McLuhan" (1995, 155). In fact, the information workforce depends primarily on a set of skills derived from verbal, cognitive, and interpersonal skills, talents that strongly influence school achievement and literacy (Baydar, Brooks-Gunn, and Furstenberg 1993). Since it is clear that a person who is information- and telecommunications-poor disproportionately lacks antecedent resources to purchase, use, and manipulate these tools to her advantage, attention to the human-capital deficit is central to a full definition of the information underclass and, concurrently, a comprehensive assault on its underlying causes (Castells 1996, 1998; Holderness 1998).

## Expanding the Definition of Information Poverty: A Periphery-Center Model

The Dickensian model adopted in much of the literature is in need of renovation. As technologies of choice are redefined, as the deployment of essential information services are subverted by technoeconomic powers, and as government plows billions of dollars into wiring public-access points, these exigencies must be incorporated into a new model of differential telecommunications access. Clearly, those who are unable to access the Internet from home represent the vast majority of U.S. households; however, distinct patterns emerge, each with its own fingerprint. Do these information sources meet the diverse needs of underprivileged residents, including ethnolinguistic minorities and disability communities, among others? Is sporadic, ad hoc access to the Internet at a library or school sufficient to develop quality skills to participate fully in the life of the community? Are we to expect the approximately one-third of Americans who are functionally illiterate to become successful Internet browsers (Kozol 1985)? These questions stretch our imagination in this arena, providing the groundwork for an expanded definition of information poverty and a rethinking of ameliorative public-policy initiatives.

I proffer a recategorization of information and telecommunications have-nots into five mutually exclusive categories, distinguished by the differential ability of participants in each of these divisions to achieve cooperative and participatory status in the social and economic life of the larger community (Sen 1992). If the linchpins of the information society, as Schement and Curtis (1995) avouch, include interconnectedness, the ubiquity or pervasiveness of information technology, and the idea of information as an item of production and consumption, then the interplay between the presence of the aforementioned attributes in the lives of persons and the absence of some or all of these features represent bright lines differentiating marginal groups (Aurigi and Graham 1998). As figure 4.1 depicts, these five groups are subsumed under three headings, existing at varied distances from the center of the information society's forces of production: individuals who are "immune to progress"; those who have "peripheral access" to advanced information and communications technologies; and "peripheral users," namely, persons who engage

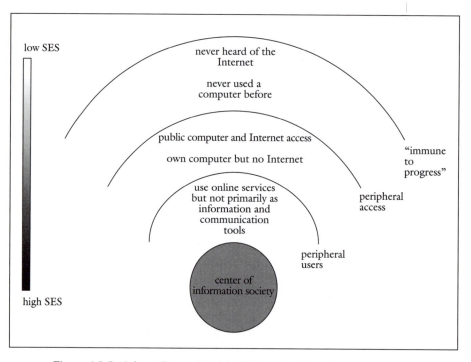

Figure 4.1 Periphery-Center Model of Teletechnology Access

in online activities other than searching or browsing for information and communicating with others via e-mail.

As the periphery-center model illustrates, those who are most completely dispossessed are farthest from the center, underprivileged in terms of socioeconomic status, technological capacity, and the possession of certain antecedent skills and talents, as well as their attitudes toward and perceptions about the information society. For example, individuals in this group are disproportionately poor; perhaps functionally illiterate; largely service workers, unemployed, or part-time workers; and have never used a computer. A substantial portion of this group is utterly unfamiliar with the Internet and may do without the most basic of telecommunications services, a telephone. Moreover, there exist attitudinal barriers, including anxiety over security, privacy, and pornography, and these concerns must be overcome before individuals in this group are willing to participate in online activities. In short, this subgroup experiences centrifugal forces, making it exceedingly difficult to gravitate toward the center. Manuel Castells's conception of the space of flows captures part of this dynamic, in articulating the logic of exclusion in the global information economy:

> Areas that are non-valuable from the perspective of informational capitalism, and that do not have significant political interest for the powers that be, are bypassed by flows of wealth and information, and ultimately deprived of the basic technological infrastructure that allows us to communicate, innovate, produce, consume, and even live, in today's world. (1998, 74)

I label this group immune to progress to imply the presence of formidable barriers impeding individuals from sharing in a larger distribution of societal benefits, including but certainly not limited to advanced telecommunications technologies. Individuals, families, and households that are marginalized from the larger society remain, as Michael Harrington diagnosed over a generation ago, "victims of the very inventions and machines that have provided a higher living standard for the rest of the society" (1962, 13).

Moving inward, away from the fringes of the information-poor, lie those with peripheral access to advanced information and communication technologies. They exist in the interstices between what Robert Reich (1997) calls "groundworkers" and "skyworkers." Reich argues that ground and sky divide the new service economy even more sharply than blue and white collars divided the old manufacturing economy. Groundworkers are described as "cashiers, fast-food cooks, waitresses, cab-drivers, janitors, security guards, hospital orderlies, retail clerks, and parking-lot attendants . . . all have been losing ground, and not even the economic expansion that began in 1991 has given them much of a boost." Skyworkers are, by contrast, "management consultants, investment bankers, computer moguls, corporate lawyers, top executives . . . in ever greater demand in the global-digital economy, selling their ideas and doing deals through the air" (7). A fairly large percentage of this group is working poor, may have a high-school degree or have attended college, and probably occupy paraprofessional, clerical, or technical positions. Persons with peripheral access to advanced teletechnologies may have access to computers or the Internet only at work or may own a computer but do not possess home-based connectivity other than a telephone. The stratum referred to as having peripheral access is qualitatively distinct from the subgroup called immune to progress: its members possess greater technology capacity, perceive the efficacy of computer networks, and have a higher socioeconomic status, affording them the ability to adapt more successfully to changing market conditions.

Finally, closer to the center of the information society are peripheral users, individuals who are middle-class, have college degrees, and work primarily in high-end service jobs (e.g., health care or business services), administration, or perhaps professional and managerial positions. Peripheral users have home-based online access, but they generally do not produce new content or knowledge; they eschew browsing the World Wide Web to find information; and they neither send nor receive electronic mail. These individuals are removed from the "power elite": they are not wealthy, nor are they likely to occupy key decision-making positions. The functions for which peripheral users employ the Internet may indeed be sufficient to meet their needs, but another stratum exists at the center of society where new content is generated and wealth created: top managers and professionals within this group drive today's productive forces and control the space of flows.

## Data and Methods

This chapter relies on data from the Tomás Rivera Policy Institute's (TRPI) Hispanic Computer and Internet Survey, conducted during the last week of February 1998. The TRPI is a public-policy institute located in Claremont, California. The survey encompasses a random, representative sample of Hispanic-surnamed adults interviewed over the telephone either in English or in Spanish, depending on their preference. The sample includes 804 respondents, and the margin of error is ±3.5 percent, which means that there is a 95 percent chance that the sample reflects the views of the Hispanic adult population within ±3.5 percent. Fifty-one questions were asked of respondents on a host of computer- and Internet-related topics, including household demographics. The advantage of surveying the U.S. Hispanic community is that a disproportionate percentage of the population tends to occupy a low socioeconomic status, lack proficiency in English, and have limited access to basic and advanced telecommunications technologies, supplying variation in poverty strata and in degrees of marginality from the information society. While this chapter cannot generalize to the entire U.S. population, the Hispanic sample provides ample evidence to explore and test the validity of the model articulated in the previous section.

The methodology has three advantages over many Internet studies. First, the sample is random, unlike surveys of self-selected Internet users. The Graphic, Visualization, and Usability (GVU) Center's World Wide Web survey (1998), for example, includes data from more than fifteen thousand unique respondents; however, it employs nonprobabilistic sampling, since there is no broadcast mechanism on the web to select participants at random. While GVU's survey is quite useful, it biases experienced and more frequent users; thus, it does not represent the complete spectrum of the Internet community. The advantage of probabilistic sampling is that one can generalize to the population as a whole rather than solely to the universe of Internet subscribers. For example, self-selection prohibits researchers from determining the characteristics of persons not using online services. Second, generalizations about the Hispanic population can be made with confidence, since the standard error is relatively small. Often in national studies that include ethnic and racial minorities as subgroups, the sample sizes are so small that the margin of error can be as high as ±9 or 10 percent, a figure that makes generalizing a tenuous enterprise at best. This sample of 804 respondents is large enough to talk about the general Hispanic adult population as well as to engage in an analysis of computer-owning and Internet-subscribing Hispanic households. Finally, the data were collected relatively recently, in February 1998. According to Birdsell and colleagues (1998), "roughly 80% of the Web-using population has been on-line for 30 months or less," which means that data collected prior to 1996 represent a fading snapshot of Internet use patterns.

The data analyzed in this chapter include descriptive statistics for the five mutually exclusive categories of information and telecommunications poverty, as described in the previous section. When differences between groups are compared, a chi-square ($\chi^2$) test procedure tabulates variables into categories and computes a chi-square statistic. This "goodness of fit" compares the observed and expected frequencies in each category to test that all categories contain the same proportion of values. All of the data used for these procedures are categorical. For example, household income is divided into three subgroups: $0 to $24,999; $25,000 to $49,999; and $50,000 and above. Educational attainment is classified as follows: less than high-school graduate; high-school graduate; and college matriculate. The data compiled in tables 4.1 and 4.2 were chosen to underscore the more striking differences among groups and are by no means exhaustive.

## A New Classification of Information and Technology Poverty

Tables 4.1 and 4.2 reveal robust differences among the three main classifications of teletechnology have-nots and between these groups and

Table 4.1  Demographic Characteristics

| | | immune to progress | | peripheral access | | peripheral use | center of information society |
|---|---|---|---|---|---|---|---|
| | | never heard of Internet (N=73) | never used a computer (N=248) | use computer only at work (N=188) | own computer, no Internet (N=140) | use online services (not for e-mail or browsing) (N=36) | use online services (for e-mail and browsing) (N=111) |
| Household income | <$25K | 81* | 71 | 46 | 40 | 28 | 20 |
| | >$50K | 4 | 7 | 18 | 25 | 28 | 41 |
| Education | <H.S. grad | 74 | 58 | 22 | 13 | 8 | 8 |
| | Some college | 8 | 16 | 45 | 57 | 81 | 76 |
| Occupation sector | professional | 8 | 8 | 35 | 31 | 44 | 45 |
| | non-professional | 55 | 59 | 56 | 54 | 47 | 44 |
| Gender | male | 47 | 42 | 43 | 46 | 58 | 60 |
| | female | 53 | 58 | 57 | 54 | 42 | 40 |
| Age (µ) | | 42 | 41 | 37 | 37 | 35 | 35 |

*All figures represent subgroup percentages. For example, the cell with the (*) is to read: 81% of those who have never heard of the Internet earn less than $25,000 annually.

(*Source:* The Tomás Rivera Policy Institute, Hispanic Computer and Internet Study, February 1998.)

households at the center of the information society. Along critical demographic, attitudinal, and cultural fault lines, significant differences exist
that suggest a segmentation of information and telecommunications
poverty in American society. It is important to note that these results do
not imply causality—in other words, technological capacity does not
explain or predict one's economic and social condition. Examining the
data through the lens of information and telecommunications access is
not an endorsement of a (soft) technological determinism. On the contrary, it is considerably more likely that a person's limited access to
advanced information commodities is due to her socioeconomic status
and resource capacity. What is claimed is that access to advanced teletechnologies is part and parcel of the set of tools with which persons ought to
be equipped to participate fully in digitally mediated political life. Along
with literacy, enumeration, and information seeking, access to and use of
advanced information and communications implements are becoming
essential. If language itself is a technology and literacy the technique
needed to master it, then how can we expect language competence without teaching literacy? If literacy takes on new forms with the advent of
new Internet-based and computer "languages," then is it not a truism
that without developing facility with these tools, a person will not possess
the techniques required to manipulate them? In short, the purpose of this
chapter is to differentiate groups among the information and teletechnology underclass, not to articulate or condone technological antidotes to
cure market inequalities.

As table 4.1 indicates, the data show dramatic differences in capacity
to achieve functioning in contemporary society by demographic characteristics. Moving across the table rows from left to right reveals
increasing affluence, educational attainment, and professionalism. It
should also be noted that the right side of the ledger is younger and
decidedly more male than those who are excluded from full participation in the information society. Table 4.2 illustrates differences in
attitudes, perceptions, language preferences, and media use patterns
among the various underclasses, data that clearly establish the periphery-center schematic as a salutary model. For example, Spanish is the
preferred language for those who are immune to progress, while individuals with Internet access overwhelmingly choose to navigate the web
in English, suggesting that ethnolinguistic barriers are integral to an
understanding of information poverty, at least for this ethnic minority.

Before we sketch a profile of information have-nots within Hispanic
households, it may be beneficial to define the technology-rich. Of those
Hispanic households subscribing to an online service, their primary uses

**Table 4.2   Attitudinal and Cultural Responses**

| | | immune to progress | | peripheral access | | peripheral use | center of information society |
| --- | --- | --- | --- | --- | --- | --- | --- |
| | | never heard of Internet (N=73) | never used a computer (N=248) | use computer only at work (N=188) | own computer, no Internet (N=140) | use online services (not for e-mail or browsing) (N=36) | use online services (for e-mail and browsing) (N=111) |
| Children's use of Internet? | play games | 18* | 19 | 46 | 40 | 32 | 27 |
| | do homework | 72 | 66 | 18 | 45 | 21 | 56 |
| Internet's primary benefit? | access to information | 21 | 26 | 47 | 50 | 50 | 56 |
| | educational materials | 29 | 34 | 22 | 23 | 14 | 14 |
| Internet's primary drawback? | kids misuse | 11 | 25 | 32 | 27 | 17 | 17 |
| | have no use | 43 | 39 | 24 | 21 | 36 | 30 |
| Likelihood to make online purchases? | likely | 23 | 21 | 27 | 23 | 22 | 34 |
| | not likely | 77 | 79 | 73 | 77 | 78 | 66 |
| What should be done about Internet indecency? gov't should | censor | 50 | 42 | 39 | 30 | 21 | 17 |
| | use blocking technology | 24 | 32 | 39 | 45 | 42 | 46 |
| Internet language preference? | English | 25 | 33 | 66 | 69 | 75 | 80 |
| | Spanish | 50 | 48 | 13 | 15 | 6 | 6 |

*All figures represent subgroup percentages. For example, the cell with the (*) is to read: 18% of those who have never heard of the Internet respond that their children would use the Internet primarily to play games.

(*Source:* The Tomás Rivera Policy Institute, Hispanic Computer and Internet Study, February 1998.)

of the Internet include, as figure 4.2 reveals, browsing for information, communicating via e-mail, and searching for educational materials, activities that seem to be hallmarks of inclusion in today's information society. Table 4.1 shows that these households are, generally speaking, upper-income, highly educated, and professional. The data also show that this subgroup is predominantly male and Generation X (Coupland 1991), and overwhelmingly prefers to surf the web in English. Aurigi and Graham define more precisely the contours of the new global information/capitalist society:

> elite groups seem likely to be the "information users" experiencing the full benefits of global, interactive telematics systems . . . there is substantial evidence that a new "transnational corporate class" is emerging which is the primary agent of operating the global economy, and which relies on intense mobility and access to interactive global computer networks on a continuous basis to "command space." (1998, 63–64)

"Commanding space" includes but is not limited to control of the space of flows that determine where telecommunications infrastructure as well as human and financial capital are to be deployed in communities throughout the United States and the world.

### Immune to Progress

The incoming tide of the information age has not lifted all boats. Among the Hispanic population in the United States, about one-tenth of household respondents have never heard of the Internet, approximately one-fifth with annual household income below $25,000 did not own a telephone in 1997 (Belinfante 1998), and fully one-third have never used a computer. Their demographic characteristics, moreover, do not indicate that they will soon gravitate toward the center of the information society, since they are subject to centrifugal forces that impede their progress. As table 4.1 shows, 81 percent of Hispanic adults who have never heard of the Internet have an annual household income below $25,000, and 74 percent do not have a high-school degree. In addition, they disproportionately occupy nonprofessional positions, mostly in service industries, manufacturing, and agriculture. The median age, forty-two, is about seven years older than for Internet-subscribing households. Finally, they are predominantly female, as opposed to Internet users, six out of ten of whom are male.

In addition, persons immune to progress remain on the periphery of society due to cultural, attitudinal, and perceptual barriers. For example, Spanish is the preferred language for a majority of respondents in this

DEMOCRACY IN THE DIGITAL AGE

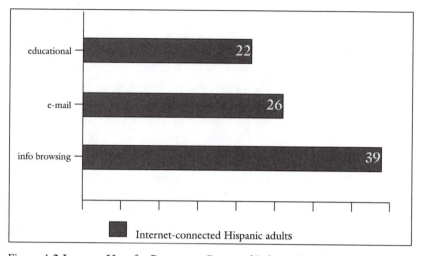

Figure 4.2 Internet Uses for Persons at Center of Information Society (*Source*: The Tomás Rivera Policy Institute, Hispanic Computer and Internet Study, February 1998)

group. While the Internet remains primarily a cultural product of English-speaking countries, with 70 percent of host computers originating in the United States, many potential users would prefer to access the Internet in their native language (see table 4.2). In addition, 43 percent of those who have never heard of the Internet and 39 percent of respondents who have never used a computer have no real need for the Internet. Corporate and media powers clearly promote the Internet as essential to the flow of social intercourse and commerce, but this manufacturing of demand begs the question of whether these technologies, as currently designed and deployed, meet the information and communications needs of individuals who have no experience with or exposure to advanced telecommunications services, a question that was addressed more directly in chapter 3. Perceptual obstacles also block persons immune to progress from wanting to use emerging media. An overwhelming majority of persons in this subgroup are unlikely to make purchases over the Internet using their credit cards, suggesting that they are far from convinced that their personal information will be secured from theft or misuse. In addition, many parents are concerned about the possibility of their children accessing pornographic web sites, and, on the whole, they possess either insufficient knowledge of or trust in blocking and filtering technologies to override their fears about potential misuse of the Internet.

*Peripheral Access*

Occupying an intermediate position between those who have never used a computer and those with household Internet access are individuals with peripheral access to advanced services. Their access is peripheral for one of two reasons, as figure 4.1 depicts. First, they may have access to the Internet in a public-access center or other non-home-based environment (in this case, at work). Or, second, they may own a computer but are not connected to the Internet. Having an Internet connection at work allows for nominal use of online services, although they are unlikely to be used overtly either for personal fulfilment or for other family members to access. Having a computer without online access means that the tool is used for word processing, spreadsheets, and household management but cannot be used to browse web pages, to distribute information, or to communicate with cohorts via e-mail. In short, individuals with peripheral access cannot (universally) avail themselves of advanced telecommunications services, such as what home Internet subscription affords.

The socioeconomic status of Hispanics with peripheral access to advanced services is substantially higher than for individuals without computer and Internet access. As table 4.1 shows, one-quarter of Hispanic computer owners earn over $50,000 per year, while the figure is only 7 percent for those who have never used a computer. College attendance is significant within this group, with over one-half (57 percent) of computer owners having attended college, compared to 8 percent of interviewees who have never heard of the Internet. In addition, the percentage of professionals among this subgroup is about one-third, four times higher than for nonowners.

Unlike the group that is completely marginalized from the information society, those with peripheral access have a modicum of experience with and exposure to computers and Internet technologies. In the first place, individuals are decidedly more comfortable with English as the Internet language of choice than are persons who are less well-to-do. According to table 4.2, of those who own a computer, 69 percent would prefer to access the Internet in English, compared to 15 percent who would prefer Spanish. Proficiency in English probably means that the World Wide Web has more to offer these individuals, as opposed to potential users who would choose to access the web in a language other than English. Second, contrary to the information-poor who find little value in the Internet (as a function of, among other things, their lack of experience with the web), Hispanic adults with peripheral access are substantially more likely to see the Internet as a valuable resource, a tool that can meet some of their information and communications needs. The latter subgroup also perceives the Internet to be an informational and recreational tool. Respondents with peripheral access are much more likely than persons immune to progress to see their children using the Internet for entertainment rather than for educational purposes, perhaps reflecting the dominant commercial and recreational currency of online services.

### Peripheral Use

Peripheral users are one step removed from the center of the information society. Approximately one-quarter of all Internet-subscribing Hispanic households use online services primarily as an information and communications resource. Individuals in this subgroup may use their computer (and modem) primarily to manage the household, to work from home, or for recreational purposes. What is striking is that the demographic characteristics of this group of peripheral users are significantly different in two important respects from those who use advanced telecommunications technologies centrally as information and communications resources. First, a substantially smaller percentage of the former group earns at least $50,000 per year. Twenty-eight percent of peripheral users earn more than $50,000 per year, compared with 41 percent of those whose primary use of the Internet is to communicate and to search for information, a statistically significant difference ($\chi^2=3.030$; $n=147$; $df=1$; $p<.1$). Another conspicuous difference between the two groups concerns their attitudes toward making online purchases using credit card informtion. Twenty-two percent of peripheral users respond that they are likely to engage in e-commerce using their credit card, while the figure for those at the center of society is 34 percent, also a significant difference ($\chi^2=2.507$; $n=147$; $df=1$; $p<.1$).

Survey respondents who use the Internet for reasons other than to communicate via e-mail and to browse the Internet for information occupy a different socioeconomic stratum from that of the typical online user. This distinction clarifies an aspect of information inequality that has only been touched on in the literature (Birdsell et al. 1998), that is, diversity in the use of and attitudes toward the Internet. While researchers have shone a spotlight on the question of accessibility to computers and the Internet, we are only dimly aware of how the Internet may be used and perceived differently, depending on one's relative marginality in the global-information economy.

In summary, accessibility to advanced information and telecommunications technologies, including the Internet, is not a function simply of having or not having a particular service or technology. The issue of access becomes a complex question, one to which policy makers must pay particular attention if they are to address seriously the inequalities that exist in the midst of an affluent society. In chapter 6 I shall once again examine attitudinal, cultural, and socioeconomic obstacles to the development of more widespread and available advanced telecommunications services, this time with respect to designing a democratic information infrastructure. In pinpointing solutions to inaccessibility to advanced services in chapter 7, moreover, I will examine how Phoenix, Arizona, is developing a community access model that is blanketing the metropolitan area with publicly available and user-friendly computer terminals, a successful civic network that, if replicated, might lift those currently immune to progress into the mainstream of the information society.

# 5

## Virtual Sounding Boards:
## How Deliberative Is Online Political Discussion?

CYBERSPACE REPRESENTS ANOTHER PLACE in which people can communicate politically. Through new venues, people can engage in many sorts of political activity, such as joining interest groups, voting in elections, or participating in political forums. Jürgen Habermas (1996) suggests civil society acts as a "sounding board" for the articulation of political issues to be addressed by government. Thus, those people who discuss political issues in cyberspace can ostensibly raise concerns and express ways of addressing these problems. Of course, political forums ought also to be deliberative, whether they be in cyberspace or face-to-face, since substantive messages must be exchanged in order for the political themes developed in civil society to be translated into items for collective action. The question for empirical research is, How useful are these virtual sounding boards in enabling deliberation in the public sphere? As a corollary to this question, What are the appropriate conditions for enhancing deliberation so these forums can more effectively inform and influence the policy process?

While many scholars and practitioners have been swept up in the euphoria surrounding the ubiquitous deployment of information and communications technologies, particularly broadband telecommunications networks, it remains to be seen how useful political forums on these networks will be for setting agendas, making public decisions, negotiating differences, and arriving at hard-fought compromises. While diversity of voices and universal service are championed as hallmarks of the public interest in U.S. telecommunications policy (Commission on Freedom of the Press 1947), the argument is proffered that these are not sufficient conditions for enabling the articulation of interpersonal, social, or political issues and concerns and that these discussions must also be deliberative. After all, promoting a diversity of voices, while imperative, does not eo ipso guarantee deliberation, negotiation, and the contestation of viewpoints (Huckfeldt and Sprague 1995). Nor is universal access to these forums sufficient for realizing a discursive, democratic polity. Deliberation or critical-rational reflection is understood to be a necessary condition of salutary political conversation online, without which digital democracy may follow the lead of "mature" media and fail to meet expectations.

While many proponents of cyberdemocracy anticipate the arrival of ubiquitous, broadband access to the home as the sine qua non of democratic reinvigoration, this indicator will not shed much light on the quality of political discourse or the propensity of participants to deliberate to arrive at their goals and objectives. As Richard Davis (1999) suggests, the video on demand and interactivity permitted by advanced networks are just as likely to allow users *not* to participate in the political process as they are to invite their involvement. Providing greater choice and opportunity only solves part of the problem of participation—for example, that related to reducing the cost of involvement—but it does not get to the heart of what motivates citizens to move from the state of disengagement to one of salutary involvement in civic life.

This chapter will proceed along the following lines. First, exploratory questions will be mapped out regarding the deliberativeness of online political forums; these research questions are to be tested empirically and clarified analytically in subsequent sections. Second, a content analysis will be conducted of a sample of political newsgroups to provide empirical validation for the deliberativeness of these new political spaces. Finally, the implications of these findings will be discussed in relation to the overall promise of cyberdemocracy.

## Exploratory Questions

According to James Fishkin (1995), the contemporary political scene is characterized by democracy without much deliberation. With the subversion of deliberative democracy by corporate powers (R. McChesney 1997b; Schiller 1996), the interests represented by various public spheres may lack the consideration and authority that are needed to affect substantively the policy agenda. As Benjamin Barber argues, "talk radio and scream television have already depreciated our political currency, and new technologies are as likely to reinforce as to impede the trend if not subjected to the test of deliberative competence" (1995, 270). But what exactly is deliberation? Fishkin (1992) tells us there are three conditions that make face-to-face deliberation possible: (1) political messages of substance can be exchanged at length, (2) there is opportunity to reflect on these messages as well as for ongoing debate and reflection, and (3) the messages can be processed interactively, with opinions being tested against rival arguments. Applied to Usenet political forums, one might expect that these three conditions could be readily met. One might even suppose that Usenet is ideally suited to deliberative exchange, since the asynchronous and virtual nature of the technology allows for reflection while its software enables participants to respond to postings and to incorporate their remarks effortlessly into an ongoing thread.

While on the face of it Usenet may appear to facilitate deliberative speech, it is necessary to explore empirically the incidence of considered, critical-rational conversation on its political forums. The interdisciplinary literature on computer-mediated communication (CMC) effects, empirical evidence from past and present cyberdemocratic experiments, and normative theorizing provide a rich set of questions for exploration. Richard Davis's (1999) analysis of Usenet groups also provides a benchmark by which the quality of online political activity can be gauged. The following queries are posed to clarify the degree to which discussion migrating to new communications networks displays or approximates any or all of the salutary characteristics of deliberation as described by theorists and practitioners.

The first research question to be addressed is, To what extent do participants of virtual political groups solely provide ideas and information versus seeking information from other forum members? There are hundreds of postings on Usenet political newsgroups every day, but, as has been suggested, the quantity of postings does not guarantee equal participation or vigorous exchange of opinion (Schneider 1996). It is vital to discern how often these postings are aimed at seeking out, acquiring, filtering, and exchanging information to increase awareness and understanding. According to W. Russell Neuman (1991), in seeking information people gather only what is necessary to make reasonable decisions on issues. If there are considerably more postings that begin and end with providing and seeking information, then it is hard to imagine reciprocal acts occurring in which participants in a political discussion articulate their interests through talking, sharing ideas, and negotiating differences.

The second research question is, To what extent do participants of political groups exchange opinions as well as incorporate and respond to others' viewpoints? As cyberdemocratic experiments illustrate, there is a tendency to substitute deliberative political discussion with "push-button" or plebiscite democracy, in which individuals register their preferences on issues without exchanging ideas or interacting with others (Arterton 1987). In effect, this portrait of direct democracy values the individual as an information provider, in registering her preferences, and discounts interaction and conversation with other citizens. While the first question addresses the extent to which participants are using newsgroups simply to amplify their own views, the second question begins to discern the extent to which political newsgroups are genuinely interactive. As Fishkin puts it, "when arguments offered by some participant go unanswered by others, when information that would be required to understand the force of a claim is absent, or when some citizens are unwilling or unable to weigh some of the arguments in the debate, then the process is less deliberative because it is incomplete" (1995, 41).

The third query is, To what extent is there in-group homogeneity of political opinion on Usenet newsgroups? Research shows that people prefer to form groups among those with whom they agree, a phenomenon known as homophily (Huckfeldt and Sprague 1995; Rogers and Kincaid 1981). In terms of the opinions fostered in these groups, social psychology research shows that in-group favoritism exists in which group members are less judgable than out-group members (Yzerbyt, Leyens, and Bellour 1995). In addition, out-group members are perceived as more homogeneous in their traits and behavior than in-group members. Homogeneity has been defined differently depending on exactly what researchers are attempting to identify. In this case, homogeneity is defined as the extent to which individual messages adhere to a certain political affiliation, defined as endorsing or supporting a political candidate, platform, issue, or ideology. In a study of political identity within British political parties, Caroline Kelly (1989) found that homogeneity was correlated with increased salience of key political objectives, such as promoting unity and strength. It will be interesting to know whether Kelly's findings are applicable to Usenet groups with well-defined agendas.

To illustrate this point, the content analysis on which this chapter is based was conducted in October 1996, during the homestretch of that year's presidential campaign in the United States. At this time there were many postings on various aspects of the candidates' character, position on issues, and so forth. However, exchanges of opinion between message posters with diverse viewpoints occurred infrequently. The newsgroup alt.politics.libertarian, for example, included scant criticism of the Libertarian presidential candidate, Harry Browne, or of the party platform. Almost every message either strongly affirmed or at least indirectly affiliated itself with the Libertarian agenda (i.e., either its presidential candidate or the party platform). In so doing, forum participants demonstrated strong in-group homogeneity. To make educated choices among political candidates, however, citizens likely need to canvass different viewpoints and assess and reevaluate their own position based on new information. This presupposes a political forum with internal imperatives for critique and discourse. Participating in forums where in-group identity is strong may truncate such an exercise.

The final question relates to the critical-rational dimension of newsgroup political discussions: To what extent are substantive, practical questions debated rationally in contradistinction to ad hominem argumentation not susceptible to criticism and grounding? This is a challenging question, since messages presenting a rational argument in some cases may not easily be differentiated from arguments in which assertions are not validated. To clarify this issue, rationality was assessed in light of Habermas's (1984) distinction among the semantic content of these expressions, their conditions of validity, and the reasons for the truth of statements or for the effectiveness of actions. In other words, the rationality of an assertion depends on the reliability of the knowledge embedded in it. Knowledge is reliable to the extent that it can be defended against criticism. Forum participants can supply reasons in defense of a certain proposition, and, to the extent that they are recognized as reasons, members can orient their actions to intersubjectively recognized validity claims. In the absence of such recognized reasons, it is unlikely that claims will be adjudicated. To illuminate this point, one forum that was examined, alt.politics.white-power, included a range of discussion describing the physical features of Africans, with some comments reminiscent of phrenological arguments of the nineteenth century. In other words, its semantic content was dissonant, unmoored to contemporary language norms. While this fact alone does not discount its potential validity, forum participants seldom advanced arguments or reasons to support their assertions, which means that the truth of their statements was not defended and made accessible to the scrutiny of the larger public.

## Why Content Analysis?

Content analysis was chosen as the appropriate methodology to address these questions. Since the deliberativeness of online political communication is really about the substantive components of messages as well as about reciprocity between message posters (also judged in this instance exclusively by examining the relationship between messages), content analysis was determined to be the tool most amenable to discoveries about the four questions enumerated in the previous section concerning: information-seeking, interactivity of opinion, homogeneity, and rationality. Content analysis is "a research technique for making inferences by systematically and objectively identifying specified characteristics within a text" (Stone et al. 1966). This methodology has been used to understand group behavior (Sproull and Faraj 1995) but not to explore the deliberativeness of self-identified political forums.

There are two principal advantages of using content analysis as the appropriate methodology for this study. First, as explained by Klaus Krippendorff (1980), content analysis is a study of data as they appear in a context, enabling one to examine extant texts. Political postings and the threads of discourse in which they are embedded comprise a defined context or horizon from which a discussion can be evaluated. It is not necessary to know who the participants are, from what walk of life they come, or with what political parties they are affiliated to paint a compelling portrait of the deliberativeness of these discussions. As Sproull and Faraj ascertain in their study of Usenet communities, "the benefits provided by electronic groups often extend beyond the direct participants when members act as conduits of information to people outside the group" (1995, 75). This generalization was arrived at not by asking message posters what they do with the information they receive via Usenet postings, but rather from the very content (or context) of the messages themselves. Of course, it is exceedingly difficult from a content analysis of messages to judge, say, the amount of time participants spend critically reflecting on other postings, either by themselves or with family and friends. This is a limitation. But as Spears and Lea argue, regarding a message as "what is made salient and meaningful in the context" rather than simply what is transmitted or omitted provides us with a "powerful and flexible theoretical tool for understanding the wide-ranging effects of CMC" (1994, 452).

Second, compared with interviews or ethnographic study, content analysis usually "yields unobtrusive measures in which neither the sender nor the receiver of the message is aware that it is being analyzed" (Weber 1990, 10). Questioning respondents or having them fill out surveys, from the perspective of content analysis, is about creating new texts, ones that are sometimes biased by the interests of researchers and the pressure felt by interviewees to supply acceptable responses. For example, a questionnaire of political attitudes may yield what are called socially acceptable responses in which respondents may exaggerate the extent to which they participate politically and deliberate on party platforms. Since participants in political forums are unaware that their messages are being studied, they are not affected by the glare of researchers and their instruments.

At the initial stage of this study, it was necessary to determine the unit of analysis to arrive at a sample frame. Since information was sought primarily on the makeup of messages, the single posting was the principal unit of analysis. Thus, a sufficient number of messages was included in the sample to generalize to their characteristics ($N$=500). In addition to the individual posting, message strings were analyzed, such as the relationship between messages, newsgroup homogeneity, and the number of threads. Thus, the newsgroup became the appropriate unit of analysis ($N$=10). In order to gauge this information, a sample of political newsgroups was selected, an appropriate number to assure that a variety of forums were analyzed but not too many to be unnecessarily burdensome to coders. These messages were drawn from Usenet political newsgroups as well as from America Online's Washington Connection. A commercial ISP was examined for two reasons: (1) to ascertain how deliberative its forums were relative to the categories described in the previous section, and (2) to determine how these discussions differed, if at all, from Usenet political forums. When the content analysis was conducted, in October 1996, there were fifty-seven newsgroups self-described as political and fourteen discussion groups on Washington Connection (see appendix B). Although many Usenet newsgroups deal with political themes, the study was limited to those forums whose addresses reflect political content and objectives.

From each newsgroup, an identical number of messages was selected for content analysis over roughly the same period of time. To be more specific, the following procedure was followed to arrive at a random sample of messages for analysis: (1) an equal number of consecutively posted messages were downloaded from ten newsgroups chosen at random (six from Usenet newsgroups and four from AOL); (2) to be confident that the sample represents the universe of messages posted to political forums, a sample of five hundred messages was needed to ensure a satisfactory confidence interval (±4.4 percent); (3) therefore, fifty messages were selected at random from ten groups for a total of five hundred messages; (4) a roughly equal time period was randomly selected to capture continuity in themes across lists. A randomly selected day and time was chosen, and messages were downloaded from each group covering approximately the same period of time; (5) to capture threads within groups, the fifty messages from each group were consecutive. To ensure that the findings were reliable, 10 percent of the messages were coded by an independent coder, once the appropriate units and categories had been developed and the coders were trained. The coefficient of reliability was found to be .84, demonstrating a high degree of interjudge consistency (Janda 1978; Krippendorff 1980).

## Content Categories

The content categories were developed to operationalize the questions posed in the previous section. It was important to ensure that the content dictionary categories actually shed light on the questions which this study aims to address. In other words, the issue of face validity was addressed by matching content definitions with the questions to be clarified, as is shown in table 5.1. The first research question, for example, asks the extent to which participants provide ideas and information versus seek information. This was measured through two specific content categories. First, the category PROVIDE was developed to analyze messages in terms of whether they involve solely the provision of information or content to the forum. Any message that involves interactivity or query was coded accordingly (e.g., as INCORP or REPLY). Of course, Usenet technology includes store and forward software, where a user typically posts a follow-up article to the entire newsgroup. Rather than coding such a message as being interactive, however, the content itself was examined. If the message made no reference to another posting and did not make queries seeking information, then it was coded as PROVIDE. The other category used to clarify this question is called SEEK; it describes only those messages that involve instances of information seeking, usually in the form of queries to other forum members. Rather than coding these two categories in terms of preponderance (e.g., determining whether a message is more about providing information or more about seeking information), a message was coded as SEEK that included any tangible evidence of information-seeking behavior. A message may have included a long diatribe on a particular political issue, but if there was at least one sentence or instance of inquiry, then it was labeled as SEEK rather than PROVIDE. A third category is a special instance of either of the first two categories in which a message provides the spark for a discussion train, known as a thread. This category is referred to as SEED, since it includes only those messages that are original, that is, preceding subsequent reply messages in time.

The second set of categories moves us into the realm of genuine reciprocity. INCORP is a category that operationalizes whether messages include opinions or ideas drawn from information sources other than postings within the newsgroup, either from expert information providers or other citizens. INCORP may also be coded as SEEK, but the reverse cannot be true. REPLY refers to a message that is a response or reply to another message previously posted. Unlike INCORP, in which a posting may include information from other sources not participating in the

Table 5.1   Political Messages Content Dictionary Categories

| Tag | Full name and definition | Face validity |
|---|---|---|
| provide | PROVIDE: a message that is solely providing information from other participants in the form of facts, opinions, and the like. | Q#1 |
| seek | SEEK: a message that includes evidence of information seeking in the form of queries, open-ended remarks, and the like. | Q#1 |
| seed | SEED: a message that plants a seed for discussion, usually providing the groundwork for a topic, always the first in a series of reply messages. | Q#1 |
| incorp | INCORPORATE: a message which includes opinions or ideas drawn from others, whether they be experts or other citizens but *not* those who are participants in the exchange in question. | Q#2 |
| reply | REPLY: a message that is the response or reply to another message previously posted. | Q#2 |
| homogeneous | HOMOGENEOUS: the extent to which the sum of messages analyzed on a single political newsgroup approach strong political affiliation on dominant or prevailing agendas, measured as mean value scored on interval scale of "extent of political affiliation." | Q#3 |
| validate | VALIDATE: an expression which is subject to criticism and grounding assessed in light of the internal relations between the semantic content of these expressions, their conditions of validity and the reasons (which could be provided, if necessary) for the truth of statements or for the effectiveness of actions. | Q#4 |
| novalid | NOVALID: an expression which presents neither conditions of validity nor reasons for the truth of the statement—instead, appeals are made largely to personal prejudice, emotion, or aesthetic judgment. | Q#4 |
| aut | AUTHOR: the mean number of authors posting per day. | |
| length | LENGTH: the mean length of a message, measured as number of words. | |
| message | MESAGE: the mean number of messages per day. | |
| time | TIME: the mean time length of a thread in days. | |
| thread | THREAD: the mean number of threads per day, a thread being a continuous discussion on a single topic or related topics occurring over a particular period of time. | |

political newsgroup in question, REPLY includes only those messages that are direct responses to previous postings.

The third question is addressed by the content category HOMOGE-NEOUS, which is a measurement of the extent of political affiliation that postings demonstrate. Political affiliation here means evidence of messages adhering to key political objectives, such as solidarity toward a political candidate, party platform, issue, or ideology. Coders assessed this affiliation based on the overall tone of the message and ranked the extent of affiliation on an interval scale (4=strong affiliation; 3=weak/moderate affiliation; 2=no affiliation; 1=weak/moderate disaffiliation; 0=strong disaffiliation). These results were summed across a newsgroup and then averaged so that a newsgroup that demonstrates strong homogeneity of opinion, such as alt.politics.libertarian, for example, would score near a four, while a political forum where there was high disaffiliation would obviously score substantially lower.

Evaluating a message based on its overall relationship with a dominant position might seem to beg the question of finding the major threads over a defined period of time. However, this two-stage approach canvasses the newsgroup for dominant themes, ideologies, or agendas and then codes individual messages as they relate to these prevailing viewpoints. By canvassing dominant threads and assessing the overall tone of a newsgroup, deductively, dominant positions or prevailing views were identified (if social identity theory is correct on the priority of in-group homogeneity, then an asymmetrical political balance of newsgroup messages should be expected). Then, in an inductive or analytic approach, each message was coded to determine the extent to which it cohered to this dominant position. While this approach is by no means fail-safe, it should provide a satisfactory indication of in-group homogeneity.

The fourth research question is answered by the content categories VALIDATE and NOVALID. Habermas attempts to define arguments that are amenable to rational agreement as holding out the premise "that *in principle* a rationally motivated agreement must always be reachable, where the phrase 'in principle' signifies the counterfactual reservation 'if argumentation were conducted openly and continued long enough'" (1990, 105). Rationality, for Habermas, is assessed "in light of the internal relations between the semantic content of these expressions, their conditions of validity, and the reasons (which could be provided, if necessary) for the truth of statements or for the effectiveness of actions" (1984, 9). In short, if postings supply reasons or arguments for the validity of their positions, then they provide the groundwork for reaching a rationally motivated agreement. If valid reasons are not advanced, then subjects, rather than exchanging validity claims, may not be able to find common ground.

The other content categories, the last five in table 5.1, are self-explanatory. They are critical for understanding how long political conversations persist, how durable discussion threads are, and the like. These content categories highlight the life cycle of discussion threads and suggest incidence of deliberation as a function of time, not just its critical-rational dimension.

Let me provide a sample message and discuss briefly how these content categories would apply. The following message was posted to the newgroup alt.politics.elections in October 1996, shortly before the presidential election:

> Bob Dole has to be the most boring, gray, uncharismatic person ever to run for president of the US. He comes across as tired, bitter and humorless. Good thing he's in between jobs. I wonder how becoming president would affect his character. A grimace would probably assume permanent residency in his face. Not that Clinton is fantastic, mind you, but he seems much more energetic and compassionate. Electing Dole would be like electing the crabby neighbor down the street.

Clearly, this message exclusively provides information to the newsgroup, primarily concerning the character and personality of the two principal presidential candidates. The author neither makes an inquiry of the newsgroup nor directly responds to another message. Of course, from the context of previous postings, it may be ascertained whether this message is indeed a response to a previous posting. However, on the face of it, this message does not meet the threshold for coding it as interactive or involving an exchange of opinions. Assessing its relationship with the prevailing theme of its thread, involving a sustained critique of Bob Dole's character and personality, reveals strong in-group affiliation vis-à-vis an evaluation of Bob Dole's candidacy. Coders scored this message as a four, which means it demonstrates strong affiliation with the in-group's agenda. In terms of the rationality of the message, it clearly fails Habermas's (1984) test of providing reasons to validate the truth of assertions made about Dole's character and Clinton's personality. These reasons may be latent and may or may not emerge if the author is prompted. For the sake of this coding scheme, if reasons are not supplied in the message itself, then its validity is diminished as a statement that would enhance the deliberative process of the newsgroup participants. Thus, this message was coded as NOVALID.

Table 5.2 Content Analysis Results

| Content categories | Political newsgroups | AOL's Washington connection | |
|---|---|---|---|
| provide | 71.2% | 67.3% | Q#1 |
| seek | 27.9% | 32.5% | Q#1 |
| seed | 15.7% | 18.2% | Q#1 |
| incorp | 52.9% | 47.7% | Q#2 |
| reply | 15.5% | 23.1% | Q#2 |
| homogeneous | $\mu=3.1$ | $\mu=3.2$ | Q#3 |
| validate | 67.8% | 75.6% | Q#4 |
| novalid | 32.2% | 24.4% | Q#4 |
| aut | $\mu=16.3$/day | $\mu=10.3$/day | |
| length | $\mu=97.3$ words | $\mu=102.5$ words | |
| message | $\mu=19.1$/day | $\mu=11.3$/day | |
| time | $\mu=3.1$ days | $\mu=4.1$ days | |
| thread | $\mu=3.7$/day | $\mu=2.6$/day | |

## The Vast Cyberwasteland?

The first question aims to clarify the extent to which political discussion in cyberspace involves information seeking, that is, the use of these newsgroups to inquire about political matters. The content analysis reveals that the bulk of political messages primarily provide a text, usually less than a hundred words, rather than seeking information from other messengers. As table 5.2 shows, slightly fewer than three out of four messages exclusively provided information to the newsgroup, while the figure is approximately 30 percent for those seeking information and less than 20 percent that are seed messages. Clearly the bulk of newsgroup postings are an expression of ideas and opinions provided to a forum. Only a fairly small percentage of messages actually seek out information on a particular topic. These postings provide a point of departure for a conversation, but if nobody responds to them, then they quickly wither on the vine.

The political forum alt.politics.org.cia, for example, was one on which postings by individuals were often long, intricate, and involved, yet there was very little questioning of newsgroup participants about particular issues. One message poster put up arcane multipage, multiseries messages on encryption, which may have been informative to a portion of the audience; however, nobody posted a response or posed a question to this gentleman. While it was a diverse forum in terms of the number of issues covered, it rarely hosted interactive exchanges.

The data support the conception of online political forums as facilitating self-expression and monologue, without in large measure the "listening," responsiveness, and dialogue that would promote communicative action, such as prioritizing issues, negotiating differences, reaching agreement, and plotting a course of action to influence the political agenda. Many postmodern writers praise the Internet as a form of self-expression for groups subordinated by the dominant culture. These activities constitute its summum bonum. The argument is made in this chapter that, in terms of the public import of communicative action, it "completes" speech, just as listening and responding to the viewpoints of others validates their utterances in the light of day.

The second question asked whether participants in political forums are incorporating the views of others in their ongoing quest for information and conversation. Is there a sense that the messages present on these forums comprise a series of conversations? Is the knowledge and information transmitted in any way discursive, geared toward coordinating action among participants? Based on this study's limited coding categories, online participants are not responding to the views of other group members. Fewer than one out of five messages represents a direct reply to a previous posting, which suggests the notion of an attenuated public sphere (see table 5.2).

In their study of six Usenet newsgroup, Sproull and Faraj found evidence for substantial social interaction, enough to evoke the metaphor of the "gathering place" to describe the contours of these social spaces. They suggest that over one-half of the messages they coded demonstrate social interaction; that is, they induce one or more replies or are themselves replies to previous postings (1995, 69). While this study accords with Sproull and Faraj in viewing virtual public spheres as fulfilling the human need for affiliation, these forums may expand free expression while doing little to solve social and political problems. The problem-solving understanding of conversation is one geared toward the articulation of common ends. The data gathered in table 5.2 do not support the problem-solving mode as the chief characteristic of online political discussion. Indeed, even the social model is an attenuated one, given that so many of the messages posted on these forums are unrequited.

If a democratic discussion is to be defined at least in part by the quality of the conversation, then the newsgroups analyzed in this study are not very deliberative. Rather than listening to others, more times than not persons opposed to a seed message used it to amplify their own views. Perhaps one reason there are so few responses is that there is no obligation to respond on the part of either latent or active forum participants

(Holmes 1997). That is to say, since messages are not addressed to particular respondents (as, say, a letter would be), there is no imperative to respond on the part of an anonymous addressee. In societies where a right of response is valued (e.g., *le droit de réponse* in France), citizens are "more than the fraction of a passive, consumer 'public'" (Derrida 1992). Where democracy is desired, there must be reciprocity. Reciprocity is unlikely in forums where participants do not feel responsible before other forum members.

With respect to question three, concerning the extent of group homogeneity, the prevailing view seems to define these forums in terms of "communities of interest," virtual gathering places in which those people who share a common interest can discuss issues without substantial transaction or logistical costs. This understanding supports the view that individuals tend to seek out those individuals (and affiliations) with whom they agree. As Huckfeldt and Sprague argue, "groups that are evenly divided in political opinion, or approximately so, must be rare. Asymmetry in the distribution of beliefs within groups is likely to be prevalent, particularly since it is known that individuals tend to seek out politically like-minded associates" (1995, 53). Testing this phenomenon reveals that over 70 percent of messages can be characterized as homophilic, that is, demonstrating either strong or moderate support for the dominant position on a political topic or candidate. The modal value for the scores was 4 and the mean score was about 3.2, which means that strong affiliation with dominant themes and agendas was evident (see table 5.2). Many forums that had a well-defined agenda revealed strong in-group identification, which means that the identity of a newsgroup is critical in understanding the extent to which it can be expected to be homogeneous.

The political forum alt.politics.libertarian was examined to explore the extent to which agreement or homophily exists on this group. If Anthony Downs's (1957) model is assumed, that persons will want to reduce their information costs by obtaining information from like-minded individuals (e.g., Democrats from other Democrats or the Democratic Party), then one would predict that this forum, dedicated to Libertarian ideology, would include a skewed distribution of viewpoints. This hypothesis was validated by content analysis of the fifty messages on this forum for homogeneity of political positions. Over 90 percent of the messages to which a political affiliation could be ascribed were Libertarian or were supportive of some Libertarian tenets. Since the content analysis was conducted one month before the 1996 presidential election, there was considerable traffic lauding Harry Browne, the Libertarian presidential candidate. There was only one criticism of Browne, from a man who believed his candidacy represented "a right-wing militia front." Notwith-standing this fact, the messenger remained committed to the Libertarian platform. The discourse on this forum was overwhelmingly hostile to government and supportive of empowering the individual, as one might expect. Oftentimes, government regulation and involvement in society were characterized as "boneheaded" or "draconian," and these com-ments were, on the whole, unopposed by lurkers who may not have possessed Libertarian predilections.

The notion that a virtual community entails the organization of people around a common interest follows from the empirical data, but the impli-cations of these findings are far from obvious. In terms of developing issues to be processed by policy makers, communities of interest may form around issues that, for whatever reason, have yet to generate sup-port in civil or political society. As Habermas points out, many issues which concern not just the problem of distribution but the "grammar of forms of life" (1987, 391–94) have yet to be adequately addressed by governmental policy, whether it be the issue of individual self-realization, quality of life, or equal rights for all groups. Communities of interest could take on the role of identifying and promoting these issues before government (Cohen and Arato 1992, chap. 10). The downside of in-group homogeneity is that it may become more difficult in an increasingly pluralistic society for new identities to coexist. As William Connolly warns, "any drive to pluralization can itself become fundamen-talized" (1995, xi), suggesting that as individuals continue to find success in affiliating with like-minded souls, their "drive to pluralization" may make finding common cause with other groups more difficult.

The final question explored the extent to which online political mes-sages are amenable to Habermas's (1984) conception of rational agreement. Of the random sample of messages analyzed, as table 5.2 illustrates, about three out of four provided reasons to justify their state-ments; the remainder of the postings did not validate or support their statements with arguments. The political forum called alt.politics.white-power included discussions of the size of the lips of Africans as well as other characteristics of minorities that several participants themselves believed crossed the line between reasoned argument and personal preju-dice. One participant called the ancient Egyptians "xenophobic," and a respondent said that his "descriptions were based on prejudices, not fac-tual reality." Another participant suggested that there is a "cephalic index" showing that the skulls of Africans differ from those of whites. A respondent asked this person if he "would care to tell us what these alleged distinctive features are and provide some evidence," but very little validation for these ideas was forthcoming. Notwithstanding the bald assertions made in this particular forum, an overall high degree of critical-rational text was evinced on Usenet and America Online (AOL) political forums. Perhaps this was in part due to the fact that users had time to compose their messages in relative isolation and anonymity. Unlike face-to-face communication, in which there is often the need to respond expeditiously to other respondents, say, in a town hall discussion, participants in online forums are not burdened to respond immediately to other citizens. They are thus afforded the time and anonymity to craft political messages that can reflect their considered judgment.

In addition to the questions enumerated above, there are important aspects of the durability of threads that are key to understanding online democratic deliberation. The content analysis reveals that a considerable portion of politically oriented messages posted to newsgroups as well as the commercial site, AOL, demonstrate attenuated, episodic, and ephemeral social interaction. Only about 20 percent of messages were actually addressed to other message posters, suggesting that sustained dialogue among all participants on a single topic or line of inquiry is uncommon. Emerging teletechnologies thus undermine severely the rhythm of democratic discourse, and this new appropriation of politics at the hands of technoeconomic powers bodes ill for the future of deliberative democracy in the years to come.

These virtual gathering places are home to an array of overlapping and short-lived threads. Participants come and go; many perhaps lurk—that is, read the posted messages without offering a testimonial. As is clear from table 5.2, on any given day there are about three separate threads or conversations occurring via political newsgroups or AOL's Washington Connection. Each thread lasts about three days on the newsgroups and about four days on the commercial network. Perhaps the threads last longer on America Online because there are slightly fewer messages posted per day. While Metcalfe's law suggests that the value of a network increases by the square of its users, the ephemeral nature of many threads is inauspicious for the formation and continuation of deliberation on a range of policy issues, since it is uncertain whether such short-lived conversations can ultimately influence what is put on the policy agenda. Although Metcalfe's law is often used to defend universal-service policies in which a network's value increases as the number of subscribers increases, the law is an insufficient validation for such a policy. While it may indeed be true that the size of the potential participant pool often is inversely related to the quality of discussion that can be achieved (Dennis and Valacich 1993), many forums consist mainly of postings that primarily provide information, a phenomenon that does not require that users exchange viewpoints and consider other opinions. Perhaps Howard Rheingold (1993) put it best when he suggested that although people might appear to be "conversation addicts," many of these gathering places seem to reflect much more talking than listening. It may be perfectly justifiable to subsidize public access to the Internet on the basis either of ensuring individual self-expression or of safeguarding democracy by creating an informed and educated citizenry; however, its benefits as a vehicle for collective action, as currently designed, may be limited (Dutton 1996).

These conclusions support Richard Davis's (1999) content analysis of three Usenet groups, an analysis of one week's worth of messages ($N$=743), downloaded, identified, and coded between June 14 and June 20, 1997. Davis suggests that Usenet "possesses certain disadvantages as a forum for public discussion of political issues. These include opinion reinforcement, flaming, and unrepresentativeness" (161–62). Davis's notion of reinforcement is referred to as homophily in this chapter, the idea being that individuals tend to gravitate to groups agreeing with their own point of view. While my own analysis does not examine flaming per se, it is clear from my coding scheme that ad hominem attacks are frequent. As Davis suggests, "Usenet political discussion tends to favor the loudest and most aggressive individuals. Those who are less aggressive risk vigorous attack and humiliation" (163). Finally, the idea of representativeness is one that I address in other chapters. Given the demographic makeup of the Internet, it is not surprising that those who engage in political activity are those who already are most likely to participate in nonvirtual civic and political life.

## Irrigating the Wasteland

The sorts of virtual political forum that were analyzed do not provide viable sounding boards for signaling and thematizing issues to be processed by the political system. They neither cultivate nor iterate a public opinion that is the considered judgment of persons whose preferences have been contested in the course of a public gathering; at least there is insufficient evidence to support such a salubrious picture of the political public sphere in cyberspace. Critics may suggest that holding actual political engagement up to the standards of democratic theory is unfair, since the way people relate to each other will only on rare occasions rival the ideal. However, it must be underscored that if cyberspace is going to be a venue for identifying, articulating, and even solving political problems, then it is necessary to discover how these tasks can be discharged. Evaluating various projects in terms of how they allow participants to solve problems as well as experimenting with new forum designs may lead to a clearer picture of the relative merits of these venues for deliberation and critical debate.

Although the drumbeat is often heard that liberal democracy is moving toward a more direct form of civic and political participation, in part due to teletechnologies that can enable home-based engagement, a wide gap exists between what can be done, technologically, and what should be done, from a political and ethical point of view. If so-called netizens have not tested their opinions in the light of day, then attenuated political discourse and push-button democracy may well represent the information age's high-water mark.

In order to enhance cyberdemocracy's potential, it is necessary to relate the findings briefly to the other characteristics of the political public sphere in order to suggest several palliatives, remedial policies to which I shall return in chapter 7. The following indicate several possible directions. In terms of the inclusiveness of these forums, universal participation cannot be guaranteed. There will always be people who are unable or unwilling to engage in the sorts of discursive practice outlined in this chapter. In addition, the anonymous nature of cyberspace creates uncertainty concerning who is actually participating. However, if the following two assumptions have merit, then the balance shifts away from who the participants are (e.g., their physical identities) and toward what they can bring to the table: (1) that ordinary people are more competent than anyone else to decide when and how much they shall intervene on decisions they feel are important to them (Dahl 1970, 35), and (2) that who somebody is remains less salient to identifying and articulating problems than what is revealed in her speech and action, for example, the content of her messages (Arendt 1958, 179). Of course, it is critical that the content of cyberspace be diverse and that universal access to these forums continue to be a hallmark of U.S. telecommunications policy. The strong correlation between socioeconomic status and ownership rates of basic and advanced telecommunications services, including computers, belie this ideal. Even if diverse groups participate in political forums, social psychology research shows that homogeneity of in-group members tends to be an important feature of minority groups, new groups, and groups with well-defined agendas, such as political groups. If norms can be established in which bridges are built connecting diverse political newsgroups, such as promoting intergroup dialogue, then at the very least the perception of in-group members toward out-groups might be changed. Another direction might be to normalize a right of reply. Perhaps the design of the network, including facilitation and moderation, can enable citizens more effectively to respond to and incorporate others' viewpoints so that collective action is as regular an occurrence online as, say, contacting the White House. These strategies will be discussed in greater detail in chapter 7 in adapting conflict-resolution techniques to political disputations in cyberspace.

# 6
# Designer Democracy

THIS CHAPTER WILL EXAMINE how the design of digital telecommunications and broadcast technologies affects the nature and scope of online activity. Design includes the architecture of a network and is implicated in facilitating or inhibiting public communication (Mazmanian, Jeffe, and Wilhelm 1995). While attention to the design of networks is a necessary condition for plumbing the democratic potential of these tools, it is far from sufficient to secure viable civic spaces. The rhetoric of neofuturists notwithstanding, it is unlikely that manipulating the design of a technology alone will have a marked salutary impact on communication in the public sphere. Since an instrumental notion of technology is so imbedded in our culture, there is often a reflexive response that manipulating communications tools—say, by providing greater bandwidth—will automatically enhance our democracy by providing interactivity, choice, and diversity of content. While this may be true, prospective participants in new virtual political activities also have the choice *not* to participate. In short, the assumption is often made that providing citizens the choice to participate via interactive services will enhance or increase participation, though the opposite is an equally likely outcome. While new technologies invite us to rethink democracy in the digital age, their design is only one component of a complex system that includes an understanding of the resources people bring to the table as well as their attitudes, behaviors, and cultural norms.

The first part of this chapter will examine how the rollout of digital broadcasting and advanced telecommunications services, such as digital subscriber lines and cable-modem connections, will likely affect the balance of democratic discourse in the United States. If set-top boxes and high-definition televisions are too expensive for many citizens, then poor households will remain in the netherworld of analog and narrowband, unable to enter the new civic spaces elite groups are exploiting to amplify their policy preferences. If the cost of high-speed telecommunications services is prohibitive for poor households, then will these technologies foster greater disequilibrium in the political system? What is more, AT&T's bid to become the largest cable company raises design issues about whether cable's closed architecture will continue to predominate in the marketplace. The high-speed service provider @Home privileges content provided by its advertising and e-commerce confederates, and content cached locally will be carried at a swifter speed than that of competing Internet providers (Werbach 1999), boding ill for the future of diversity and debate online.

The second section will explore the issue of digital redlining and the bypassing of low-income and minority communities in central cities and rural areas of the United States. Existing data on competitive local exchange carrier (CLEC) deployment of fiber optics reveal that the near-term prospects for home-based connectivity of advanced telecommunications services are dim in many central cities, communities of color, and rural regions (Aufderheide 1999, Lilley 1998). The third section of this chapter shifts to examine the development of public access points for disadvantaged residents and communities, designed to improve economic viability, to spur aggregation of demand, and to enhance the civic and educational life of all people. National policy has centered on deploying advanced telecommunications services in public institutions, such as libraries, schools, and community centers. The last section will provide a cautionary note, warning against unwittingly creating dual standards of political incorporation.

## Becoming Digital:
## The Prospects for Home-Based Cyberdemocracy

American society is becoming digital at a brisk pace. The analog world is fading away, to be superseded by a digital world in which the functionality of telephones, computer networks, and televisions is multiplying. Of course, these devices will continue to be used primarily for nonpolitical purposes. The telephone will continue to be used to carry on private conversations (Fischer 1992). Computer networks will be used to relay information of a social nature (Sproull and Faraj 1995). And the television, however sharp its picture, will be turned on primarily to beam "breathless, slick entertainment" into the home (Gitlin 1993). A Benton Foundation poll (1999) released in January 1999 found that the public, while viewing television as principally an entertainment medium, did support the educational, civic, and social potential of the medium upon closer examination. Eighty percent of respondents, for example, believed that broadcasters ought to support public television. While there are many American residents who do not know what digital television is all about and who are also unaware that broadcasters receive their license for free, once they are informed about these matters, their opinions reflect a concern that broadcasters do more to promote the public interest. Thus, the initiation of a novel telecommunications or broadcast tool into the larger society provides an opportunity to reassess its purposes, particularly as a tool potentially supportive of democratic activity (R. McChesney 1993).

## Digital Television

Digital television is the latest information and communications tool to be laureled, following in the tradition of radio, analog television, cable, and the Internet. In April 1997 the Federal Communications Commission allocated 6 MHz of additional spectrum to incumbent television stations in order to transmit digital television signals. This new spectrum capacity can be used in various ways by broadcasters, including any of the following: (1) the development of one or more high-quality signals with crisper pictures and CD-quality sound; (2) multiple signals superior to today's analog signals so that broadcasters can engage in multiplexing; (3) so-called premium services such as subscription television, pay-per-view, and audio signals; and (4) nonbroadcast services such as data transmission, paging, or wireless services. The result of this spectrum allocation means that it will be technically possible and socially desirable to provide broadcasting green spaces for noncommercial purposes, establishing unadulterated political and public forums in which citizens can express ideas and concerns. One could imagine in the best of all possible worlds a democracy channel in which citizens and noncitizens alike could access information on a host of hot-button political issues, convey their opinions to officeholders, engage in lateral exchanges of ideas with other interested participants, and become better informed on the major issues of the day. One could also imagine attention paid to local expression in which content would be provided by local organizations, grassroots interest groups, and concerned citizens. This sort of engagement at the neighborhood level—if designed in a provocative manner—might widen the circle of formal and informal political participation. This digital broadcast channel would be supported by a public television fund and undergirded by community partners who would provide quality content to local audiences.

These vignettes may seem idealistic in an environment in which broadcasters largely decide how spectrum is used. A casual review of the history of the public-interest standard—from its origins in the Radio Act of 1912 to the present day—will reveal that its heyday was in the mid-twentieth century, while the last two decades have witnessed its debasement at the hands of laissez-faire proponents. The world of analog broadcasting is ending with a whimper and not with a bang, and reconstituting a robust public interest standard in the digital age will require a herculean effort. Remarking to the International Radio and Television Society that "only the private sector can develop content" for digital broadcasting, FCC chairman William Kennard (1998) reflects the distance we have wandered from any trenchant public standards. As Robert McChesney suggests, "one of the most striking developments of the past decade has been the decline of public service broadcasting systems everywhere in the world" (1997a, 1). To believe that only the private sector can develop content is to deny human expressiveness, the diversity of high-quality content produced every day by public-service media, nonprofit groups, artists, and ordinary citizens who express themselves in interesting ways yet who have no major distribution outlets to amplify their voices. The world of multi-casting, moreover, will require effective community alliances to fill channel capacity in a way that meets a wide range of community needs (Somerset-Ward 1997).

Notwithstanding these less than optimistic observations, Ruth Teer-Tomaselli (1996) and Douglas Kellner (1998) provide ample evidence for vibrant public-service media in which the expression of voices and the airing of programs from members of the community are taken seriously by the viewing public. Indeed, one could argue that it is essential for government to support political broadcasting and public-affairs programming, however rare and however poor their ratings (Garnham 1990). The private sector may be the primary producer of content, but much of this programming provides ample divertissements for the public and little support for republican government. The trusteeship obligations of broadcasters are predicated on the assumption that the diversity of voices mentioned earlier will never receive equal allocation of spectrum; thus the term "station owner" or "broadcaster" is synecdochic for the public as a whole, in its role as producer of content, as expressive agent.

In 1934 statutory mandate in the United States said that broadcasters must serve the "public interest, convenience and necessity," and the 1946 Blue Book as well as the 1960 Programming Policy Statement underscored the national commitment to political broadcasting, local self-expression, and public affairs programming (Krasnow 1997). The Blue Book stated unequivocally that "the public interest clearly requires that an adequate amount of time be made available for the discussion of public issues" (Kahn 1973, 208). And the 1960 Programming Policy Statement lists "Public Affairs Programs" and "Political Broadcasts" among those elements usually necessary to meet the public interest (246). In the late 1970s and early 1980s FCC chairman Mark Fowler emphasized that he would take a "marketplace approach" to broadcast regulation. Subsequently, the FCC eliminated rules and policies that quantified the extent to which for example broadcasters ascertained community problems, provided nonentertainment programming, and kept detailed program logs. While the public-interest standard was reaffirmed in the 1996 Telecommunications Act, it is far from clear what teeth it will have in an era of converging technologies and proliferating channel capacity. How will the public interest be applied, for example, when Internet companies and broadcasters merge or when the latter have the capability to broadcast six channels?

It is against this backdrop, in which spectrum scarcity regulation and the trusteeship model are for all intents and purposes in abeyance, that in October 1997 President Clinton convened his Advisory Committee on Public Interest Obligations of Digital Television Broadcasters (PIAC) to ascertain in a new media environment what the public interest should encompass. In PIAC's final report, *Charting the Digital Broadcasting Future*, released in December 1998, the exploration of public interest obligations vis-à-vis political communication was gravitating toward broadcaster commitment to voluntary provision of free airtime for political candidates. The core recommendation of the advisory committee in improving political discourse pinpoints "candidate-centered discourse" as integral to the public interest, suggesting that five minutes per night be set aside for the thirty nights before an election so that candidates can relay their messages to the potential electorate. As the final report states: "there are creative ways to improve political discourse, provide opportunities for candidates to get their messages across to voters and to enhance voter understanding without heavy monetary costs to broadcasters, regulation of the content of programming, or without it being a kind of programming that will cause viewers to turn away" (Advisory Committee 1998, 59). Broadcasters would be free to determine the format of candidate discourse, and the five minutes need not be contiguous. Deciding which candidates to feature on the air would also fall to broadcasters, who could choose to highlight major candidates or a particular party's candidate without having to allot equal time to alternative viewpoints.

Following almost a year of deliberation from advisory committee members, panel presenters, and public comment—all supported with piles of reports and pamphlets detailing their respective positions—these recommendations regarding political discourse are insufficient to meet the needs of a democratic society. In contradistinction to the potential inherent in digital television, recommendations for voluntary, candidate-centered discourse seem unlikely to invigorate civil society—that is to say, enhance the quality of political discourse among citizens, provide venues for public production and expression of political content, and integrate marginalized and apathetic citizens and noncitizens into the process. As Ruth Teer-Tomaselli pointed out in her 1996 Spry Memorial Lecture, "I take the purpose of public service broadcasting to be the provision of a universal service of excellent programming, while maintaining public legitimacy through an editorial independence from both the government of the day, and rampant commercial interests" (1996, 1). Empowering civil society, including use of broadcast media to amplify these voices free from government and industry pressure, allows for ideas and preferences to bubble to the surface that address unresolved problems in U.S. society, ones that incumbent political parties and commercial interests may choose to ignore or suppress (Cohen and Arato 1992).

During the second advisory committee meeting in December 1997, a panel called "Perspectives from the Public Interest Community" was convened expressly to address the question, How can digital broadcasting enhance democratic processes? The panelists were unanimous in viewing digital television as roughly a means of shifting the focus of political discourse in civil society from elites to ordinary citizens. Mark Lloyd, director of the Civil Rights Forum, raised the issue of whether "all citizens will be able to participate effectively in the political process [or] have access to public space" (1997, 15). For Lloyd, what makes television a powerful tool for democracy is not so much augmenting the power of entrenched political parties but in providing channels for "authentic community voices." This vision of the public interest in telecommunications is a far cry from the nostrum of amplifying candidate positions on issues on a voluntary basis, situating political power in local communities and concerns. Lloyd laments, among other things, the loss of ascertainments, that is, local network affiliates actually finding out what the important local issues are and creating television programs about these issues. Challenging local broadcasters to "find the director of the local senior center, and head of the local YWCA, and the local union leader, and the director of the local medical center, and other community leaders, and give them the microphone," Lloyd suggests that these public-interest standards are more rigorous than five minutes a night of candidate-centered discourse, and he underscores the need for station owners to be obliged to set aside civic space for the public to discuss public-affairs issues.

As Andrew Schwartzman, president of the Media Access Project, suggested in his panel remarks: "between the two it is the rights of the viewers and listeners, and not the broadcasters, which are paramount" (1997, 19). Self-government is not so much about deciding between major political candidates, as Schwartzman contends, but about the flourishing of diverse voices and airing of common concerns for resolution by the political process. Given that television and radio are such ubiquitous media and given their prominent role in "informing" the public, for better or worse, their potential impact on edifying political life cannot be underestimated. However, since the debate over public-interest obligations has shifted in recent years toward the side of broadcasters, it is unlikely that we will witness a return to ascertainment and equal-time regulations without robust public pressure that articulates and acts on specific media-reform efforts.

One of the more intriguing recommendations of the advisory committee was the call to create a new noncommercial channel that would provide educational, civic, and multicultural programming to communities. The idea is that once the commercial broadcasters return their analog spectrum, sometime before 2006, part of it—the equivalent of 6 MHz in each market—would be reserved for the creation of this noncommercial channel in each market. Rather than providing national programming that is divorced from the interests and issues animating local communities, the noncommercial channel would be predicated on the establishment of partnerships—including schools, libraries, museums, social-service organizations, and public service media outlets—in order to serve each viewing community. Such a channel would be bolstered by a trust fund that would be derived from auctioning the remainder of the analog spectrum or from fees broadcasters will have to pay to use their additional channel capacity for pay-per-view services.

While the proposals outlined in this section would augment greatly television's potential to serve the public interest, unless they are taken up by Congress and the FCC there is little hope that digital television will be anything better than a convenient diversion for viewers. Spearheaded by Mark Lloyd at the Civil Rights Forum, a coalition called People for Better TV formed in May 1999 to pressure FCC chairman William Kennard to start a proceeding regarding what digital broadcasters owe the public in return for use of public property, the airwaves. The coalition, which includes a phalanx of civil rights groups, pediatricians, consumer and women's groups, as well as religious organizations, argues that the PIAC recommendations provide a point of departure for an open process through which the public can express its ideas and preferences. Such a process would go a long way toward defining what the public interest entails in turn-of-the-century America, hopefully preserving and extending the progressive notion of media as a vehicle for social progress.

### Advanced Telecommunications Services to the Home

The Telecommunications Act of 1996 calls for the promotion of advanced telecommunications capabilities in a "reasonable and timely fashion," such services being defined under §706 (c)(1) as "high-speed, switched, broadband telecommunications capability that enables users to originate and receive high-quality voice, data, graphics, and video telecommunications using any technology." The rationale for legislating advanced service delivery involves promoting the public interest, including enhanced educational content delivery, promoting public health through telemedicine, and encouraging electronic delivery of government services. The Alliance for Public Technology (APT), an industry-backed advocacy organization dedicated to promoting advanced universal-service goals, contends that achieving universal access amounts to a "prerequisite for equalizing opportunities in every . . . sphere of living—economic, political, educational, or social" (Alliance for Public Technology 1998a). Over the past several years, the locus of the universal-service debate in the United States has shifted from preserving and promoting plain old telephone connections to extending this concept to broadband services.

Organizations and individuals who share APT's vision assume that political rewards will follow for citizens who can access these technologies. The examples proffered are of people downloading political information on candidate positions, party platforms, campaign contributions, and the like while also discussing issues with other interested participants in public forums. The problem with this archetypal vision is that it tends to exemplify or reify the life of the new professional classes, while it does little to explain how persons currently outside the political system will be encouraged to participate via this medium. As Manuel Castells suggests, digitally mediated life will likely "expand through successive waves, starting from a cultural elite, [which] means that it will shape habits of communication through the usages of its first-wave practitioners" (1996, 360). The examples of salutary use of information and communications technologies continue to pertain to more affluent persons, frequent voters, and other elites who are the least in need of innovative policy initiatives to ensure their access to and use of new media. Uses of advanced services such as educational content delivery, lifelong and distance learning, and job placement and welfare-to-work programs would add value to the lives of underskilled and underemployed Americans, fortifying the ground on which they walk.

The future of cyberdemocracy appears deferred given the heavy-handed involvement of untrammeled economic and commercial interests in deciding the fate of technologies putatively valuable from the point of view of extending opportunities for political involvement to a larger segment of U.S. society. The values being promoted in the debate over the functionality of advanced services should not be largely elite values, those derived from the upper stratosphere of American society. If we are to believe David Resnick, political life on the Internet already resembles business as usual, and we are entering an era in which "cyberspace simply becomes another arena for the ongoing struggle for wealth, power and political influence" (1998, 54; also Davis 1999). Designing a democratic telecommunications infrastructure—one in which the general population has a stake—remains a story in search of a broader audience, one that extends beyond university and corporate walls. As Jacques Derrida asks, "how then to open the avenue of great debates, accessible to the majority, while yet enriching the multiplicity and quality of public discourses" (1992, 100)? Without open platforms and democratic media this debate never really commences; it is like an M. C. Escher sketch in which ascending and descending amount to the same activity, and all stairs lead back to the same point of origin.

## Bypassing Poor Neighborhoods, Communities of Color, and Rural America

Manuel Castells's notion of space of flows captures much of the dynamic occurring in the United States (and around the world, for that matter) regarding the deployment of telecommunications infrastructures. As Castells puts it:

> Under the new, dominant logic of the space of flows, areas that are non-valuable from the perspective of informational capitalism, and that do not have significant political interest for the powers that be, are bypassed by flows of wealth and information, and ultimately deprived of the basic technological infrastructure that allows us to communicate, innovate, produce, consume, and even live, in today's world. (1998, 74)

Over the past decade in the United States, for example, telecommunications networks have been built linking up valuable places, in business centers and affluent residential enclaves, often selectively circumventing neighborhoods and other regions that are undesirable from a market point of view. As the Alliance for Public Technology stated in its comments in response to the Federal Communications Commission's Notice of Inquiry concerning §706 of the Telecommunications Act, "APT fears that service providers in their quest to gain market share will neglect all but large businesses and other affluent customers to the detriment of ordinary residential and rural customers" (1998a, 1). Indeed, since the telecommunications industry was deregulated in 1996, eyebrows have been raised over the mergers and obvious strategies of players to "cherry-pick" their competitors more lucrative markets in order to maximize profits (Aufderheide 1999). The advertising slogan of the new MCI WorldCom, proclaiming that the "world is officially open for business," is undermined by empirical evidence illustrating that large segments of inner-city and rural areas are being bypassed in the deployment of fiber-optic networks. In neighborhoods already experiencing massive human-capital deficits, including the disappearance of gainful employment (Wilson 1996), circumventing these communities means businesses become even less competitive, further depleting the barrios and ghettoes of resources as businesses are forced to relocate. Households meanwhile cannot access the key information and services that can augment their prospects for economic, educational, and political success.

William Lilley, president of InContext, Inc., a Washington, D.C., consulting company that performs political-economic analysis, has developed sophisticated graphs illustrating the deployment of fiber-optic backbones in central-city areas of America's largest metropolitan regions. What the maps reveal is that low-income and minority communities are being bypassed in the provision of fiber-optic networks by competitive local exchange carriers. Whether it be Albuquerque, Seattle, or Washington, D.C., a similar dynamic is at work. First, telecommunications service providers will often target large businesses in the central city's financial and commercial areas. When competitors roll out their facilities to go toe-to-toe with incumbent carriers, they often deploy their fiber-optic trunks alongside their competitors to attract the same high-end customers. Once high-rise buildings in central cities are served and the market is saturated, competitive carriers will stretch their facilities to edge cities, such as Bellevue and Redmond, Washington, home of high-tech business clusters. Once these deployments are made, there is no backtracking to poor neighborhoods. In these and other large metropolitan areas in the United States, with commercial districts and affluent communities receiving the bulk of fiber deployment, communities of color and low-income residents are largely seen as valueless, that is, unable to provide a return for investors. Rural Americans are also underserved, as industry complains that it is unprofitable to serve remote communities. The effective truth of this asymmetrical deployment of advanced telecommunications infrastructure is that large and successful businesses are able to reap the rewards of information technology—in the form of economies of size, research and development, and so forth—thus gaining a competitive advantage over businesses that are unable to link up with these important networks. Similarly, residents living in affluent neighborhoods are able to benefit from high-speed connections to the Internet at lower cost—online access that can amplify their ability to engage in digitally mediated economic, social, and political activities. Access to these services will undoubtedly translate into a greater edge for those already advantaged in society.

The incumbent carriers match their competitors by offering digital subscriber line services over existing telephone lines. Cable operators, meanwhile, are rolling out broadband services with upgraded cable-modem connections that pass, as of April 1999, approximately fifteen million households. According to an Aspen Institute report, by the year 2002 we can expect high-speed connections to be commonplace. Capabilities of 6 Mbps will allow for full-motion video, paving the way for the convergence of voice, video, and text at prices around what people now pay for cable television service (Aspen Institute 1999, 3). While the Aspen Institute working group, including industry leaders, bases its forecasting of broadband rates ($30/month) on a per-home cost of installing 5+ Mbps capacity at $1,000, and a reasonable time to allow capital recovery, others see the future in less optimistic terms. With AT&T's $58 billion offer for MediaOne, Mark Cooper of the Consumer Federation of America suggests that this equates to $5,000 for each of MediaOne's cable television subscribers. To recoup its investment, AT&T will need to compete for premier subscribers of telecommunications services, while low-end customers will be squeezed (Farhi 1999). It also means that capital investment in infrastructure will occur in well-heeled communities, while cable broadband rollout will be deferred for low-income and rural customers.

Faster digital telephone lines are also coming on line from companies in certain parts of the country and in certain communities. Many rural communities will probably not see digital subscriber service for some time to come, however, due to the high cost of providing these services and market imperatives that translate into competition among cable operators, competitive carriers, and incumbents for high-end business and residential customers. They will likely remain on the periphery without vigilant government monitoring and even intercession where appropriate.

These services are also priced at rates too high for poorer households to afford. Depending on what part of the country a person inhabits, the monthly rates are high for swift downstream capacity, and one-time charges may include service connection, a digital subscriber line (DSL) modem, and an Ethernet card. According to the FCC, residential penetration of broadband services, either from cable television or telephone companies, is less than 1 percent of households as of early 1999, and the current $50–$60 monthly basic service for DSL will be prohibitive for many low-income and rural households that happen to be offered the services in the first place (Federal Communications Commission 1999).

## Public-Access Workstations and Community Building

The empirical data and forecasts presented in the previous sections suggest that home-based cyberdemocracy may well remain out of reach of many U.S. residents for the foreseeable future. The Alliance for Public Technology suggests that "the 'digital divide' is widening and threatens our nation's future unless the [Federal Communications] Commission fully and promptly implements Section 706" (1998a, 4), but these remarks notwithstanding, it is unlikely in an era of deregulation and relative government impotence in implementing far-reaching public policies that §706 will apply to underprivileged households in society for some time to come.

In lieu of home access, the Federal government has initiated a series of programs aimed at ensuring that all persons have access to advanced telecommunications services, whether it be in a schoolhouse, a library, or a community center. Beginning in the Clinton administration's early years, the U.S. Department of Commerce's National Telecommunications and Information Administration (NTIA) was tasked with devising mechanisms by which public institutions would be outfitted with the latest telecommunications tools, as recipients of either competitive grants or preferential rates. In its *White Paper on Communications Act Reforms*, released in January 1994, the administration set out as a goal the linking of all classrooms, libraries, hospitals, and clinics to the National Information Infrastructure (U. S. Secretary of Commerce 1994, 5). The notion of universal service proffered in this document included, among other things, the seeds of the NTIA's Telecommunications and Information Infrastructure Assistance Program (TIIAP) as well as the e-rate program, a universal-service fund that provides preferential rates for schools and libraries to build a modern telecommunications infrastructure.

In the same year the *White Paper* was released, the thirty-six-member U. S. Advisory Council on the National Information Infrastructure was formally established and appointed by then–Secretary of Commerce Ron Brown. The advisory council provided direction on the development of the NII in its *Kickstart Initiative* report. The report states unequivocally that the way to build out the nation's telecommunications infrastructure is to interconnect public access points so that all persons can participate in communications networks:

> The best approach for this Nation is to bring the Information Super-highway to the neighborhood. That is most rapidly accomplished through connecting schools, libraries, and community centers where everybody—young and old, rich and poor, those with and without dis-abilities—can obtain affordable access to the Superhighway. (1996, 7)

Clearly, the national government has tended to view connecting America as a task involving linking public-access points to advanced information and communications technologies, thereby building community. The advisory council and the administration speak with one voice in lauding the benefits to society as a whole from meeting their goals and following their strategies for realizing ubiquitous communications technology deployment. The report is eerily silent about achieving home-based access to advanced services, and notwithstanding telecommunications reform legislation pending at the time of the report's release in Congress, the tenor of the *Kickstart Initiative* centers on public infrastructure development as the sure mechanism to provide access and thereby rein-vigorate communities.

As the 104th Congress was winding up in late 1994, passage of telecommunications reform seemed a fait accompli. On June 28, 1994, the Democrat-controlled House of Representatives passed two measures revamping the Communications Act of 1934, each passing with only four and five dissenting votes, respectively. Despite this near-unanimous sup-port in the House, the Senate was unable to muster key Republican support for S1822, a bill sponsored by Ernest Hollings (D-S.C.) that included, among other things, up to a 5 percent set-aside of pipeline capacity for noncommercial applications. In a September 23, 1994, press release, Republican Senator Bob Dole (R-Kan.) lambasted the Hollings bill, suggesting that its "major problems included its approach to univer-sal service, its excessive regulation, its protectionist domestic content provisions, and its outlandish, if not unconstitutional, 5% set-aside requirements."

The Clinton administration was either extremely prescient concerning the backlash telecommunications reformers would experience (i.e., with potential campaign contributors) or unable to connect its own work with the NII advisory council to broaden universal-service goals. Clearly, establishing a federal-state board to develop ways to ensure low-cost phone service for the poor was part and parcel of telecommunications reform; yet a comprehensive link was never made between these (potentially) disparate goals. As has become clear in retrospect, with the passage of the 1996 Telecommunications Act, §254 and §706 are linked—albeit tenuously—to the extent that §254 provides a stepping-stone for deploying advanced telecommunications services, while §706 (and subsequent clarifications by the FCC) remains foggy in addressing specific mechanisms by which advanced services will penetrate the home (beyond regulatory forbearance). Indeed, the FCC has unwittingly created two universal-service funds—one to provide discounts to schools and libraries and the other to support high-cost and poor residential customers—that compete for political and public support in an era in which these universal-service funds are made transparent, thus susceptible to the "no-new-tax" rhetoric of conservative politicians.

One problem the Clinton administration faced early on was how, in an era of deregulation and government downsizing, the executive department was to encourage widespread deployment of services with limited allocations of resources. After all, telecommunications services, as well as the human training and support necessary to make these programs effective, are extremely expensive. Schools and libraries are hard-pressed to find room in their budgets for hardware, and local governments were unsure how streamlining service delivery and allowing citizen-to-citizen and citizen-to-government online exchanges would burden already overloaded city staff. The Telecommunications and Information Infrastructure Assistance Program (TIIAP) was the answer to these concerns. An initiative begun in 1994 to promote the widespread and efficient use of advanced telecommunications services in the public and nonprofit sectors, TIIAP has awarded, since its inception, over $118 million in matching funds, monies spurring nearly $280 million in total investments. Perhaps the animating idea driving the program, as stated in the preface to its *Lessons Learned* report (U. S. Department of Commerce 1996), is that "TIIAP has made a special effort to encourage and to award projects that help to reduce the considerable gap between the information 'haves' and 'have-nots.'"

Among grant winners over the past five years, several projects have advanced cyberdemocratic objectives in enabling citizen access to government information and services as well as a more direct voice in what is put on the public agenda. In the city of Phoenix, Arizona, a project called

"Phoenix at Your Fingertips" was broadened in scope in 1995 with the infusion of TIIAP (and matching) funds in the amount of $571,925. The aim of the grant was to target the city's underserved populations. This program will be discussed in greater detail in the next chapter, particularly the way in which it has addressed the issue of differential access to advanced telecommunications services.

Another major federal initiative to expand public access to advanced telecommunications technologies is the e-rate program, a program that provides schools and libraries with discounted telecommunications services (i.e., telephone service, satellite transmission, pager services, e-mail), Internet access, and installation of internal connections, such as classroom- or schoolwide networks. Discounts for eligible schools and libraries vary from 20 percent to 90 percent on the cost of telecommunications, with the greatest discounts going to schools and libraries serving the highest percentage of poor students. In particular, discount levels are determined by the percentage of students who qualify for the National School Lunch Program. E-rate funds are derived from charges recovered from interstate telecommunications carriers. The discounts are used to reimburse vendors providing schools and libraries with these technology services.

In the first year of the program, the Schools and Libraries Division (SLD) of the Universal Service Administrative Company received over 30,000 applications for funding from schools and libraries, a figure that increased to 32,000 in the second year's application cycle, ending April 1999. During the 1998 funding period, $1.67 billion was allocated to 25,785 applicants, a quarter of total funding going to schools and libraries with poverty levels of 75 to 100 percent in a given community. Year-two applications represent a funding demand figure of $2.435 billion, a figure slightly higher than the legal limit for e-rate funding, $2.25 billion. Thus the demand for telecommunications services—for building out a basic telecommunications infrastructure to meet the needs of the information society—remains high, and the e-rate is one important universal-service mechanism for mitigating the social divide that results from unequal access to information technology.

The e-rate program has provided telecommunications services, internal wiring, and Internet connectivity at lower rates for poor urban school districts with severe human and social capital deficits. According to a report published by the Education and Library Networks Coalition (EdLiNC), an umbrella group of school and library associations promoting the e-rate program, called "E-Rate: Connecting Kids and Communities to the Future" (1999), the Chicago Public School District, which serves 430,000 students on 559 campuses, received $47.5 million in funding in year one, support that allowed the district to bring the Internet into at least one classroom in every one of the district's schools in that year. In Louisiana, the $500,000 in e-rate funding received by the State Library of Louisiana in 1999, combined with $2 million in state funding and $7 million from the Gates Library Foundation, means that this money can be leveraged to provide a meaningful public telecommunications system, with the concomitant professional development, labor-intensive mentoring, training of end users, and content development that will maximize the utility of the network.

While these programs begin to lay the groundwork for a public telecommunications system, what is clear is that these public and private ventures are dramatically underfunded and woefully insufficient to provide low-income and minority communities quality public access to advanced information technologies. If the goal of the administration is to build human capacity, aggregate demand for advanced services, and seed community development, then these programs only partially succeed in fulfilling that mission. Every year, for example, the TIIAP program is assailed by political powers in Congress who view the program as frivolous. They claim that rather than the public sector spending millions to jump-start a handful of technology-enhanced programs across the nation, the government ought to get out of the way and let the market perform its magic. Fortunately for the program, it is usually salvaged due to the intervention of Nebraska senator Bob Kerrey, among others. The $18.5 million allocated for fiscal year 1998, for example, amounts to an average grant of $402,173 for each of the forty-six winners, an ample seed grant but perhaps insufficient to sustain a program and build the capacity of its staff and target users (usually disadvantaged residents). The e-rate program has also been under assault. It has been subject to numerous delays, legal challenges, government preaudits, and claims of being overly bureaucratic. Representative W. J. Tauzin (R-La.) constantly seeks to strangle the program, introducing legislation to reduce e-rate funding to a level appreciably below demand for services.

Now that schools and libraries are finally being connected, these hardware needs scarcely begin to address the resource deficits faced by the worst-off public institutions. One program to be examined in the next chapter, the U.S. Department of Housing and Urban Development's (HUD) Campus of Learners program, is one that addresses the human-capacity needs of end users, issuing a contract among housing authority residents to become lifelong learners, including building their literacy and skills to become competitive in the job market. All told, these programs have one Achilles' heel: none addresses sufficiently the human infrastructure issues without which no program will be successful. If we want to enhance participation in civil society as well as formal political participation, then it is not enough to build a modern telecommunications infrastructure. If we focus solely on bandwidth and megabytes rather than on how these tools are to be implemented to redress human-capital deficits, then the e-rate will succeed in providing boxes and wires to schools and libraries, as promised, but it will not enhance palpably the performance of students.

The administration's early vision of community infrastructure development reinforcing human-capital development was a sound concept in an age in which valuable skills, resources, and literacy are in short supply among many U.S. residents. A vision of raising all boats with the incoming tide is admirable, but if it is not properly funded and viewed more comprehensively, then we risk creating two classes of citizens, one relegated to public access, the other enjoying the benefits of home-based information and communications services. If properly supported, public institutions can build human capacity, creating computer-enhanced learning environments where citizens and noncitizens alike can perhaps for the first time in their lives learn about the public sphere and political society and through this introduction (and intervention) become more attuned to how political participation can benefit their own lives.

## Opening the Space of Flows

Earlier in this chapter, I discussed Manuel Castells's notion of space of flows as an important heuristic in grappling with the bypassing of low-income and rural residents and communities of color in the provision of advanced telecommunications services. Castells's argument is that "the new society," predicated upon knowledge and organized around networks, is "characterized by the structural domination of the space of flows" (1996, 398). These information flows are organized around command-and-control centers able to coordinate and manage the new linkages constantly joining the system. There are several nodal centers in the United States and globally that organize these flows, and most of the major metropolitan areas in the United States contain miniconcentrations of flows, usually in financial centers, around which a technocratic-financial-managerial elite coalesces and dense information networks are formed.

While it is true that the network society as it now exists gravitates to valuable places from the perspective of informational capitalism, one hopes that network architecture will remain dynamic, open, and interoperable.

Of course, the accumulation of wealth and property remains a function of global financial markets and their networks of management, but the open platform of information access bodes well for those persons on the periphery of society. Circumventing those areas that are perceived to have little or no market value may be a reflexive occurrence for industry, but public and private actors working in concert can open new spaces for exchanging "value" where value is not limited to the icy calculus of self-interest and financial gain, such as the social value inherent in increasing the number of users on the network. Taylor and colleagues (1996) document the application of information and communications technologies to local and national government. Bryan, Tsagarousianou, and Tambini (1998), moreover, see in the ideology of the civic networking movement a force to contravene the dominant logic of the marketplace. Across America small communities are aggregating demand to build infrastructures where industry would not otherwise have ventured.

In the mid-1990s, citizens of Bologna, Italy, came face-to-face with the issue of how to value the importance of computer literacy and connectivity to the exercise of political citizenship. The city's civic network, called IperBolE, was being developed, and network designers as well as the community had to decide the extent to which there ought to be a right to connectivity in Bologna. Part of the debate over network architecture revolved around the political value of a network to which only a small segment of city residents could have access. How valid would, say, polling and voting referenda be if results were based on responses from a self-selected and demographically skewed portion of the public? As Damian Tambini suggests in his case study of the IperBolE network, "Bologna demonstrates that some [state] intervention may be necessary for the useful application of CMCs in democratic processes. This case further demonstrates that the possibilities for civic networks are completely altered when the right to connectivity (as an ideal, but especially as a reality) comes into play" (1998, 107). In the next chapter I will present a case study of Phoenix, Arizona, and suggest how this city network aims to open the space of flows. As with Bologna's civic network, the conscious effort to extend the city's reach to encompass all of its residents is one example of how social exclusion is not inevitable under the logic of space of flows. As long as the morphology of networks is fluid, concerted public and community action can open these flows, providing benefits to those persons otherwise immune to progress.

# 7

## Catching the Red Queen:
## Public-Policy Renovations

IN LEWIS CARROLL'S WONDROUS *Through the Looking Glass*, Alice finds herself in a country ruled by the Red Queen, a place that challenges Alice's assumption about progress. Rather than actually moving from point A to point B upon running fast, Alice finds herself where she began, a very strange occurrence indeed to someone coming from a perspective in which running implies movement across time and distance. A brief exchange between Alice and the Red Queen highlights their incompatible Weltanschauungen:

> "Well, in *our* country," said Alice, still panting a little, "you'd generally get to somewhere else—if you ran very fast for a long time as we've been doing."
>
> "A slow sort of country!" said the Queen. "Now *here*, you see, it takes all the running *you* can do, to keep in the same place." (147)

This phenomenon, referred to as the "Red Queen effect," subverts our traditional notion of progress, a broad worldview inherited from the Enlightenment. The Red Queen forces us to reflect on these principles as well as the empirical reality of contemporary life in which so many people in America struggle to keep pace in economic (Blackburn, Bloom, and Freeman 1989), social (Case and Katz 1991), and political life (Verba et al. 1993).

This chapter will suggest ways in which the Red Queen effect can be mitigated. The diffusion of new technologies in general and information and communications technologies in particular oftentimes exacerbates inequalities in society, including political inequalities. The Internet, for example, amplifies the voices of those who are already advantaged, since regular online users strongly correlate with likely voters, heavy campaign donors, and so forth (Bimber 1998a, 1998b; Davis 1999). If the market were left to its own devices, then these services and commodities would remain more or less in the hands of the most affluent households and communities, and the less fortunate would run faster only to remain on the periphery of society (Castells 1998; Dahl 1996). The causal priority of education, parent involvement, lifelong learning, social environment, and literacy, outlined in chapter 3, suggest ways in which the Red Queen effect can be mitigated. However, ameliorating these human-capital deficits may be easier to do on paper than in an environment hostile to large-scale policy initiatives, particularly those that challenge the autonomy of the marketplace. Other changes, such as modifying the culture of the Internet by instituting new rules of order, may not require the redistributive and regulatory arms of the state but do demand that people alter their perceptions, attitudes, and behaviors in order to foster tolerance and respect for others' viewpoints.

Four public-policy renovations will be described in this chapter, each of which addresses the enhancement of one of the features of digitally mediated political life explored in the previous four chapters. The metaphor of the Red Queen will be used to suggest that unless comprehensive and redistributive policies are enacted along the lines advocated in this chapter, inequality, poverty, and social exclusion will continue to plague American society in the coming years. There will be the appearance of progress, but the underclasses will not move anywhere (Economic Policy Institute 1999). In the first section, I will apply John Rawls's (1993) concept of the difference principle to U.S. telecommunications policy. Rawls's principle states that inequalities in liberal regimes are to be tolerated to the extent that those who gain more from the division of basic goods ought to do so on terms that improve the situation of those who have gained less. This principle will be applied to the differential distribution of antecedent resources affecting participation in digitally mediated political life.

A corollary to this first point concerns the movement of U.S. society toward universal participation in virtual political life. The notion of providing public points of access for disadvantaged residents will be analyzed in the second section, and lessons will be derived from a case study of the Phoenix at Your Fingertips civic network. Citizen-to-citizen and citizen-to-government political interactions in publicly accessible venues will be highlighted—in particular, the city's efforts to extend to underserved residents of Phoenix ubiquitous, well-supported access to these networks. As long as centers are within short distance for residents, whether on foot or via public transportation, these institutions, such as community centers and libraries, can assist residents in meeting their information needs. These needs encompass not just short-term information needs but also more comprehensive skill and literacy deficits, the development of which can lead to persons becoming more likely to participate in political activities (Rosenstone and Hansen 1993).

The third section will provide solutions toward enhancing deliberation in online political forums. This section will explore several strategies for improving the quality of online political dialogue based on the adoption of certain conflict-resolution techniques to cyberspace. To develop public spaces that engage in problem solving and negotiating collective action, the following three strategies are offered: (1) instituting a right of reply so that participants in a dialogue are obligated to validate and defend their ideas against criticism, (2) encouraging moderated panels in which facilitation can occur to provide organization and direction to otherwise rudderless discussions, and (3) facilitating interforum dialogues in which in-group members are compelled to consider alternative viewpoints as foils to their own.

Finally, the prospects for political multicasting and public set-asides with the dawning of digital television provide a window of opportunity to ensure that political broadcasting, local self-expression, and public-affairs programming are construed as part and parcel of the public interest in communications. Several ideas will be canvassed to ensure a strong democratic component to emerging information, communications, and media technologies, such as obliging broadcasters to convert a portion of commercial channel capacity to public-interest purposes. In addition, it is necessary to establish a predictable funding mechanism to support public-interest content, perhaps predicated on a fee on the gross revenues of broadcast, cable, and satellite operators.

## The Difference Principle

The differential access to and use of advanced information and telecommunications technology undoubtedly reflects deeper structural flaws in unfettered market capitalism (Soros 1998). As Robert Dahl underscores, "market-oriented capitalism generates initial inequalities in access to potential political resources, including money, wealth, social standing, status, information, coercive capacities, organizations, means of communication, 'connections,' and others" (1996, 646). While third-sector involvement, governments, and strong communities can modify these inequalities, the extent and direction of change may depend on forces that have been in abeyance in the United States for at least a generation or more, such as faith in the efficacy of government and the presence of social democratic parties in power.

In his second inaugural address, Franklin Roosevelt made the radical assertion that "the test of our progress is not whether we add more to the abundance of those who have much; it is whether we provide enough for those who have too little" ([1937] 1996, 131). President Roosevelt's address subverts the juggernaut of progress, typical of advanced capitalist countries, in which the diffusion of novel technologies and soaring financial markets are primary hallmarks of progress. Esteeming the contributions of all residents of society, including the poor, and developing public policies that ensure that the deleterious effects of market inequalities are mitigated are values captured in John Rawls's "difference principle." Rawls suggests that an ideal form for the basic structure of society should be established in light of accumulated results of ongoing social processes, outcomes including the accretion of gaping inequalities. Rawls believes that rational people would agree to equal divisions of basic goods; however, inequalities would be tolerated insofar as "those who have gained more than others are to do so on terms that improve the situation of those who have gained less" (1993, 282). The difference principle is meant to apply to the main public principles and policies that regulate social and economic inequalities but should not imply continuous correction of particular distributions and private transactions.

If this principle guided the promulgation of laws, surely the Telecommunications Reform Act of 1996 would not have passed muster. Several years after its passage, Public Law 104-104 has not brought more competitive rates to residential customers (Center for Media Education 1998; Cooper 1998, 1996); the most vulnerable network users are not experiencing better services (Aufderheide 1999); and meanwhile several larger telecommunications companies are orchestrating colossal mergers in order to preempt competition (Barker and Barber 1998). A procompetitive regulatory environment has yet to be reconciled with universal-service policy, in part due to the fact that certain telecommunications companies have shirked their responsibility in preserving and promoting universal service while interlopers cherry-pick the choicest business and residential customers.

One saving grace of the act is the Snowe-Rockefeller provision of the 1996 Telecommunications Act (the so-called e-rate provision) permitting deep discounts for schools and libraries in low-income and rural communities to connect to the Internet. Discussed in chapter 6, the e-rate warrants another mention, since, as originally conceived, it exemplified the difference principle: interstate telecommunications providers, in return for relaxed regulatory restrictions and greater profits, were to contribute to a new universal-service fund from which the poorest and most rural of schools and libraries would receive a substantial share of these monies in the form of deeply discounted telecommunications products and services, including telephone services, e-mail, and Internet connectivity. This means-tested program targets those institutions and communities in greatest need, thus fulfilling a vital public interest in ensuring that the weakest links in American society can connect to the information highway.

The program, however, has been besieged by key decision makers in the public and private sectors who see more parochial gain in disparaging a program that promotes the well-being of geographically isolated and low-income U.S. residents. While the e-rate grant program is far from perfect and offers only peripheral access to advanced services, it reflects a commitment to a just and equal social order, to equal educational opportunity for all. Of course, a more comprehensive attack on the problem, as Michael Harrington (1962) stressed in his work on poverty, will more thoroughly assail the predicament of persons immune to progress. If policy makers measure progress in part by the effects it has on the worst-off in U.S. society, then we might expect a reversal of fortunes for those among the ranks of the information and telecommunications underclass (Economic Policy Institute 1999).

The periphery-center model of information and communications poverty presented in chapter 4 revealed significant differences among subgroups, each distinguished by its technological capacity and use, socioeconomic status, and perceptions and attitudes toward advanced services. The affluent society composes a minority culture, if measured by technoeconomic prowess; hence the new underclass cuts a wide swath, including individuals who may not normally be considered marginal. Those with peripheral access occupy the ranks of the information underclass, because many in this group may lack a foothold in the global information society given the ephemeral nature of their skill sets, their underrepresentation in higher education, and their ad hoc access to advanced telecommunications services. A marginal investment in programs benefiting those in the interstices of the information society would most likely provide a substantial return for society as a whole. Opportunities and resources ranging from greater state and federal investment in vocational, technical, and job training; legislation offering tax credits to purchase personal computers; and scholarships to women and minorities to pursue science, math, and computer-related disciplines would most assuredly stabilize the ground on which they walk.

Those who are entrenched in information and telecommunications poverty clearly require a more substantial investment in infrastructure, education, and social support to assail its underlying causes. Offering more GED classes, life-skills development, basic keyboarding, and word-processing applications in communities with numerous accessible public workstations would be ameliorative. Those community technology centers located along public transportation routes and offering child-care services are often the most popular. In sharp contrast, in Houston, Texas, the fourth-largest U.S. city, there are virtually no community centers with computer workstations and Internet connections, and only a few of the public libraries have installed publicly accessible terminals to provide access, particularly to the 20 percent of residents who live under the poverty level. A plurality of individuals in this subgroup cannot see beyond the horizon of their everyday experiences to harness concrete applications of new information and communications technologies. Also, since these individuals have never used a computer, navigating its interface may seem daunting at first blush. Indeed, their experience runs counter to the cultural dogma of the information society, summed up in Microsoft's advertising slogan "Where do you want to go today?" From the vantage of many of America's poorer residents, the two qualities endorsed in the message, mobility and direction, are out of joint with their daily experiences. Notwithstanding the ubiquity of computer networks and the Internet in the United States, they have not always mollified the isolation and disaffection felt by many poor people (Castells 1998).

Several strategies involving public-sector leadership and greater private-sector investment can mitigate the cultural, perceptual, and attitudinal barriers an alienated underclass may experience. The language barrier facing many U.S. residents—whether their primary language is Spanish, Vietnamese, or Tagalog—will remain as long as content is provided almost exclusively in English. Information as essential as the voting ballot must be printed in languages other than English when greater than 5 percent of citizens in a precinct comprise a linguistic minority, according to the 1965 Voting Rights Act (§4). Why cannot other essential information be electronically available in languages other than English? Public and private actors should focus on creative uses of spectrum as well as substantial means of financing ownership of media outlets, new and old, by underrepresented ethnolinguistic minorities, African Americans, and women.

Undoubtedly community investment is key to building human capital, and this will come as distressed urban and rural communities are viewed by investors as potential "new markets" rather than as blighted neighborhoods. In July 1999, President Clinton announced a new plan to provide tax credits and loan guarantees for investors, to enhance their likelihood of doing business in impoverished areas of the nation. Combined with funds in the U.S. Department of Education budget for community technology centers and support for neighborhood empowerment and enterprise zones, this new markets approach may contribute to reversing the space of flows of financial capital and infrastructure development that Castells asserts will circumvent poor and minority communities.

Also, industry, community-based organizations, and state and federal agencies need to assuage anxieties about online content through outreach to parents about the efficacy of filtering and blocking technologies, since many parents living in poverty who have no exposure to the Internet tend to be overawed by reports of its unwholesome aspects (Turow 1999). Finally, industry must provide assurances to online users regarding the security of personal transactions. These strategies do not necessarily involve substantial outlays on the part of stakeholders. Of course, it is also true that these palliatives are probably not sufficient to alter materially the status of many disaffected residents.

Undoubtedly, to expect a marked reduction in the ranks of the information and telecommunications underclass requires substantial investment in low-income and minority communities. As Michael Harrington suggested almost forty years ago, "a campaign against the misery of the poor should be comprehensive. It should think, not in terms of this or that aspect of poverty, but along the lines of establishing new communities" (1962, 178). Today, people's imaginations drift to the thought of technology enabling virtual communities that will ostensibly provide the sort of mobility and control to enhance the prospects of the poor (Shapiro 1999; Dyson 1997). However, this approach is oversanguine and usually technology-driven, deflecting attention away from the development of people and their talents (see Webster and Robins 1998). As John Kenneth Galbraith argues, for example, "the myopic preoccupation with production and material investment has diverted our attention . . . from the greater need and opportunity for investing in persons" (1958, 257). What was true in the 1950s and 1960s remains true today: political leaders and the mass media consistently ballyhoo investment in emerging technologies as an anodyne to economic, educational, and social problems, while downplaying the building of human and social capacity. Without antecedent resource development as a stepping-stone to bring disadvantaged residents into a technology-reliant age, to muse about political incorporation in civil society for the poor is to inherit the wind. Building telecommunications and human infrastructure ought to be a two-pronged approach, working in tandem so that users sitting in front of computer terminals are confronted with the best-trained staff and themselves have the talents to navigate information critically to meet their diverse needs.

### Nueva Mara Villa: A New Campus of Learners in Los Angeles

One solution (and by no means a sufficient solution) to these entrenched skill and resource deficits—shared by Harrington (1962) and Galbraith (1958), among others—is to alter the social reality or environment in which the poor are mired, for example, through creative solutions to housing problems. The U.S. Department of Housing and Urban Development (HUD) developed an initiative called the Campus of Learners whose mission is "to transform selected public housing developments in cities across the nation to campuses where every resident is pursuing educational opportunities." Some campuses house learning centers where residents take computer classes, improve their language proficiency, develop life skills, and take GED classes. It must be underscored that the Campus of Learners initiative provides a learning environment in which residents agree to contract with housing authorities to enroll in an educational program as a condition of living on campus. This contract governs the relationship between residents and the housing management division, such that residents are encouraged to spend part of their day as learners, mastering today's technologies within the context of lifelong learning and practical, transferable skill development. Cultivating a learning environment where one's environs are altered empowers local communities by giving them the tools they need to become economically self-sufficient. Given what Manuel Castells (1996, 1998) tells us about the logic of space of flows in a networked society, these communities would otherwise be bypassed in the deployment of valuable telecommunications, financial, transportation, and employment links. However, the program was never properly funded and has been put on hold indefinitely, which is quite unfortunate given the promise it holds to transform the ethos of the inner city into a dynamic, networked learning environment.

Just to provide one example of the potential of programs like the Campus of Learners, in September 1996 two sites in the county of Los Angeles, under the authority of the Community Development Commission (CDC), were selected among twenty-six sites nationwide to be designated as Campuses of Learners. As Carlos Jackson, executive director of CDC, expressed, "the Campus of Learners initiative was a challenge to transform public housing into safe and livable communities where families undertake training in new technology and telecommunications." One of the sites, Nueva Maravilla, is 93 percent Hispanic, and almost one-half (48 percent) of its residents are eighteen years of age or under. Ninety-one percent of the residents, moreover, have an annual income below $20,000. IMAGE 2000 Family Learning Centers provide Internet access and telecommunications links with local colleges and universities, local school districts provide on-site adult education computer courses, and the Los Angeles County Public Library undertakes English and Spanish literacy and English as a Second Language educational services.

While the Campus of Learners designation has perhaps provided an identity and mission for an overarching technology-intensive, human-capacity-building initiative, its benefits do not include cash grants from the federal government to hire new staff, train existing staff, or procure much-needed hardware and software. Instead, the CDC has patched together funds from state programs, such as JTPA, to sustain its initiatives. This program has garnered so much attention not because these residents are using advanced telecommunications technologies to engage in the political process. This task is dwarfed in comparison to developing life-management skills, meeting basic needs, building workforce skills, and finding employment. This said, residents are developing the antecedent skills and capacities that undergird (online) political engagement. One must learn to walk before running. These programs need to be funded in accordance with the difference principle, whether it be fees returned from the telecommunications industry, a surcharge on related services, or general revenues. The e-rate program, already mentioned, provides discounts for hardware, but the human-capacity building and human-infrastructure development are vital and require funding at a level equal to or exceeding that for hardware. Unfortunately, Nueva Maravilla is not eligible for e-rate discounts, so it must generate the funds for costly telecommunications services and equipment from other sources.

Education program specialist Rosa Medina of the County of Los Angeles Housing Authority stresses that the needs of residents outstrip the ability of staff and volunteers to meet their significant human-capital and life-management needs, particularly child rearing for young women and workforce development for men (interview, October 16, 1998). Without sufficient funding and support, residents cannot expect to have the social contract met, since there are simply not enough educators on staff to meet the needs of learners on the campus. If the campus's social contract is to be met by the federal government and housing authorities, then they must be able to provide an environment in which every resident has the opportunity to develop her latent talents. Since so many of us—private citizens, shareholders, and large businesses—benefit from the deployment of advanced telecommunications services, it is just and prudent (and consistent with the difference principle) to provide a fund to make these lifelong-learning opportunities true beacons of hope for the most disadvantaged in American society.

## Toward Ubiquitous Deployment of Advanced Services

The Nueva Maravilla program, along with others scattered across the nation, reach only a small segment of the population. These successful programs ought to be replicated and adapted to local exigencies, but this will take substantial societal investment. In an era in which most social programs are shrinking and folding into public-private ventures, the prospects for expanding innovative programs, such as Campus of Learners, are not good. However, if there is one saving grace in federal funding for social programs, it is the universal support for education and technology programs that seems to cut across political dividing lines. Perhaps one of the central challenges of the coming years will be to capitalize on the success of programs with a proven track record in meeting community needs by garnering the political support to replicate these programs across the nation. If a program is working in Los Angeles, then it may be transferable to El Paso or Detroit, and policy makers ought to attempt to seed similar programs rather than reinventing the wheel or deploying and developing redundant infrastructures.

### Phoenix at Your Fingertips: A Case Study

One program that has achieved success in addressing disparities in access to advanced telecommunications services is Phoenix at Your Fingertips, a civic network developed in Phoenix, Arizona, aimed at enhancing citizen-to-citizen and citizen-to-government engagements. Sprung from the confluence of several key actions on the part of city officials in the early and mid-1990s, Phoenix at Your Fingertips solves several of the key issues of access in America's metropolitan regions, given what we know to be the case about the deployment of broadband services by certain segments of the telecommunications industry (chapter 6). The Information Technology Management Department (ITMD), a small outfit made up of city personnel from several Phoenix city government departments, was established to set up citywide standards and the necessary information technology infrastructure to attempt to coordinate already decentralized technology in a decentralized government. The efforts of this task force were acknowledged and merged with management information systems (MIS) to form the basis of a new unified vision of the delivery of technical services as well as to provide a unified delivery of electronic services to the citizenry of Phoenix. In the first place, an electronic community-access model was established (ECAM), a vision for a one-stop information source with a consistent, user-friendly interface.

At about the same time, city manager Frank Fairbanks was assembling an Information Superhighway Task Force, made up of staff from multiple departments, challenging administrators to envision how the city could participate in the information superhighway. The city of Phoenix's *Information Superhighway Task Force Report* provides an overarching vision for the city's information and communications technology goals, including supporting critical social, political, economic, and cultural objectives. The National Information Infrastructure concept, conceived in the federal executive department, had taken root by this time, and cities were hoping to design information systems and civic networks that provided some of the benefits promised in the original (federal) vision statements. The task force described the mission, policy, and goals that would animate the city's new information technology infrastructure. Among these goals was the recognition that although the private sector would support many of these services, it was the responsibility of city government to promote universal access and equity of service as well as the public right-of-way. According to Kristine McChesney, assistant information technology director, the electronic community-access model included, almost reflexively, a universal-service paradigm: "universal service was one of those things. It needed to be. It was part of the culture of the city that it would be part of [the ECAM model]" (interview, October 5, 1998).

This concern for universal access and equity in service has played a starring role in the subsequent development of the Phoenix civic networking vision. As is clear from figure 7.1, the initial information superhighway vision, as it applied to the greater Phoenix metropolitan area, was to augment ECAM with an Electronic Village concept. The Electronic Village was built into the original vision and was meant to supplement the defects of any city-supported system. The idea of the Electronic Village was "to enhance Phoenix's sense of place and community by creating an environment . . . where citizens can participate in government, business, social, leisure, and community activities using various means of electronic communications" (Information Superhighway Task Force Report, 1995, 25). It would go beyond ECAM in two important ways. First, it would not be confined to the Phoenix municipal area; rather, it would encompass much of Arizona and concern broader issues of self-governance. Second, the roles assumed by the Electronic Village would be broader than those the city was willing to address. For example, the city's calendar of events, one of the more popular sites on PhoenixNet, is limited to city-sanctioned events. The Electronic Village would have no such restrictions and could freely post events and issues voiced by the community.

These two visions, working in concert, strive to meet the needs of municipal residents. There were really three barriers to be overcome to

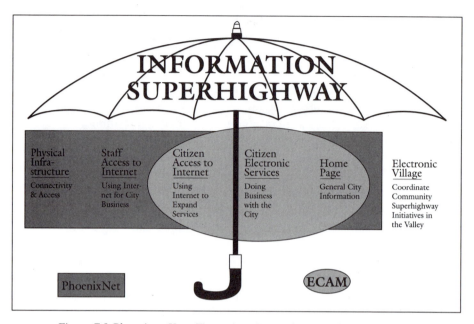

Figure 7.1 Phoenix at Your Fingertips: Overarching Goals (*Source*: City of Phoenix)

provide more ubiquitous access to the network. First, the geographic iso-lation of underserved communities was of overriding concern to city officeholders. Rather than marketing the network and hoping the com-munity would come to a few central nodes, the city strove to reach the places where poor and disenfranchised residents coalesce, including fam-ily centers, career service centers, and the like. In 1995 the city received a grant to provide computer workstation access to citizens of Phoenix, regardless of their age, class, or geographic proximity to the city center. The U.S. Department of Commerce's TIIAP grant allowed for the installment of public workstations, to be positioned within a three-mile radius of virtually every Phoenix neighborhood. By October 1997, as fig-ure 7.2 shows, a total of fifty-six workstations had been installed at thirty-seven sites, including libraries, community centers, senior centers, and nonprofit agencies. Once the original plan of geographic dispersion had been met, the city redoubled its efforts in bringing the civic network to the heart of disadvantaged neighborhoods, locating workstations in family centers and other venues familiar and accommodating to residents.

The second barrier to be hurdled was the fear and intimidation many residents experience in interfacing with the machines. The city's strategy for mitigating these concerns was twofold. In the first place, the user interface was designed from the user's vantage point. According to a

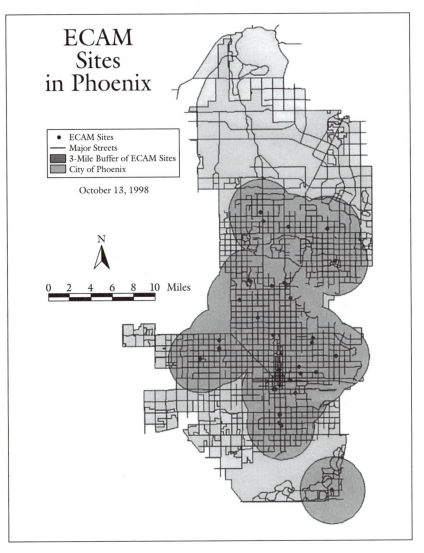

Figure 7.2 Toward Universal Public Access in Phoenix (*Source*: City of Phoenix)

recent report by the National Telecommunications and Information Administration highlighting its TIIAP grant recipients, called *Lessons Learned*, "The Phoenix project stands out for the extent to which it presents the information in a user-friendly manner. In its service, bureaucracy has disappeared, and information is presented in categories . . . that everyday citizens can readily understand" (U. S. Department of Commerce 1996, 21–22). Rather than organizing municipal information under department headings, online databases are organized by topic so that they reflect the end user's information-seeking behavior rather than that of service providers.

The other way to make accessing electronic services second nature to citizens is to employ library staff and senior citizens to help demystify this mode of receiving, gathering, processing, manipulating, and sending information. Historically the mission of the library has been to assist patrons with their information needs, including moving users toward greater self-sufficiency by mastering search engines and databases. Since Phoenix public libraries were already experimenting with providing electronic services in their domain, it was a natural partnership to work with the Information Technology Department to overcome the negative perceptions of electronic services, manifested by, among other factors, people's lack of experience with and exposure to the technologies. In addition, most of the citizen outreach and training came from senior citizen volunteers at the senior centers. Over twenty-four thousand volunteer hours were accumulated and served as the bulk of the match for the TIIAP grant.

Finally, hardware problems have been tackled by supplementing the civic networking model with the Electronic Village concept. As noted, there are limitations to city-run information services, including constraints on posting content provided by independent service providers such as community organizations and not-for-profit organizations. Government agencies are also restricted in placing city-sponsored workstations in churches, synagogues, and mosques due to First Amendment restrictions. The Electronic Village concept complements the civic network, as figure 7.1 suggests, uniting the best of government services, however restricted, with content and services generated at the grassroots level. The Electronic Village Coalition is an umbrella organization comprising multiple cities, not-for-profit organizations, and private partners, including certain Internet service providers, whose mission is to generate electronic networks from the bottom up. The aim of the coalition is to work in coordinated fashion to reach universal access in the community. Putting this mission into practice by recycling computers to outfit new workstations at low cost, the coalition also works with staff to conduct training and on-site troubleshooting.

One functionality that the Electronic Village Coalition and PhoenixNet are working toward is moderated community forums and facilitated online dialogue. The Phoenix civic network has embarked on an ambitious plan to promote online dialogue on important public policy issues, such as mass transit and air quality. This feature, called Phoenix Forum, is in its early stage. The Phoenix Forum works through participation by city staff, public officials, and other forum hosts, including private sponsors, who post information on a topic on the network and then solicit input from citizens. Designated facilitators on the network review public comments, and the most pertinent responses are posted on the forum site. It should be underscored that this is not an open forum, where citizens are free to air any comments they may choose while responding to the postings of fellow forum participants. Experience to date in Phoenix has revealed very little real interest among staff to sponsor these types of forums. City and county agencies experimenting with these unfettered, interactive forums were rather disappointed, having received few useful responses from interested residents.

What the city learned was that the promotion of cyberdemocracy takes time. Indeed, in the case of Phoenix, the most-utilized information services are those dealing with job opportunities and training. Many Phoenix residents, citizens and noncitizens alike, will not necessarily go to public terminals to access public forums or chat lines; rather, they frequent career, community, or senior centers primarily to accomplish certain practical tasks, such as resume building, job searches, and welfare-to-work transitions. This said, it is much more likely that the greater the benefits and opportunities users see in the technology, beyond finding a job or using Microsoft Office, the greater their chance of staying on the network to widen their circle of participation in other activities, including political dialogues and exchanges. The most successful workstations have been those installed in community, career, and senior centers, since residents come to these venues with specific tasks to perform. If these terminals are to be used by underserved clients for political purposes, as defined broadly in this book, then they will probably be side effects of these initial, nonpolitical uses, perhaps following on from successful first contact with these information and communications technologies.

In the future, as Kristine McChesney suggests, the hope is "to see technology become a more integrated way of doing things, so citizens think to do things electronically first" (interview, October 5, 1998). With the Electronic Village concept more fully integrated into the civic network, McChesney sees greater regional cooperation and coordination, so that Arizona residents can tap into existing services in a convenient environment. Of course, one pitfall of privileging online access to government services at the expense of print materials is that not all residents of a community have access to terminals to take advantage of these services. In addition, for a city such as Phoenix, which has a growing Hispanic population, there is an increased need to provide electronic and print information in Spanish as well as English. The city currently lacks the capacity to provide the network in two languages. Thus it remains the domain of English-speakers. The city has applied for grants to begin to address this problem, but it will probably remain a hurdle for some time to come.

## Enhancing Deliberation in Online Political Forums

The risk of new technologies—such as the Internet, high-speed broadband services, and digital television—becoming rampant features of information exchange and communication is the fear of push-button democracy becoming the norm in the twenty-first century, not so much as a formal process of national referenda but as a bastardized version of (manufactured) consent, generated by public-relations experts and entrenched political machines bent on swaying public opinion to meet objectives that are often parochial, shortsighted, or private (Schiller 1996; Chomsky 1993). There is a certain superficiality built into the very exercise of public opinion—often unreflective and knee-jerk in quality—a feature that Jean-Jacques Rousseau noticed long ago when he described public opinions as "very mobile and changing . . . like the dice which leave the hand" ([1758] 1960, 74). Unmoored, unreflective public opinion is easily manipulated and changes swiftly, depending on the flow of events, often as they are packaged and amplified by mass-media outlets.

Freedom of speech and its manifestation in online gathering places often reinforces the notion of public opinion as instant feedback and off-the-cuff expression, since expression is often equated with democracy, debate, and the exchange of viewpoints. However, free speech is a necessary but insufficient condition for such political activity. As Nicholas Garnham suggests:

> while the rights to free expression inherent in democratic theory have been continually stressed, what has been lost is any sense of the reciprocal duties inherent in a communicative space that is physically shared. I think two crucial duties follow from this. First, there is the duty to listen to the views of others and to alternative versions of events. Second, participation in debate is closely linked to responsibility for the effects of the actions that result. (1992, 368)

Garnham identifies two features of political debate in which duties have been forsaken in a rights-based culture. These deliberative features of political participation, as discussed in chapter 5, are often missing or in short supply in online political activity where the need to express oneself and to bond with others in like-minded communities, however precious, takes priority over "reciprocal duties" of listening and taking responsibility for one's participation. Garnham's urgent message requires creative design solutions and changes in online etiquette that may move us toward more accountable and civil online political behavior.

While the clarion call is often heard that the Internet is a technology that can overcome many of the problems inherent in an unequal social order—particularly due to its ability to make possible decentralized and interactive political activities—a nagging issue for society relates to the displaced and disembodied nature of these (virtual) social interactions that threatens to exacerbate the erosion of a deliberative and reflective political public sphere. In a fascinating article, David Holmes suggests that rather than hailing the Internet as a radical departure from the world of broadcasting, we ought to view it instead primarily as a deepening of the social experience sired by television. Holmes contends that the outcome of Internet interactivity has fostered an augmented "communicative abstraction" (1997, 30), that is, a mode of social interaction in which the valence of social meaning is determined increasingly by the "screen culture" of television and the World Wide Web. For Holmes, broadcast television was the progenitor of a new lifestyle where familiar landmarks derive from television personalities and advertising slogans at least as much as from face-to-face interactions in physical space. Amplifying Jürgen Habermas's notion of the structural transformation of the public sphere, from one based on a critical reading public to one based on a mass public of culture consumers, Holmes suggests that "the greater the dependence of the individual on television, the less dependent she becomes on the public sphere which is being displaced in practice" (34). I will return to Habermas's analysis in the next section, but for our present purposes it is necessary to show how Holmes's analysis suggests that newer, interactive technologies may contribute to rather than abate the disappearance of the public sphere.

Central to Holmes's concern is the deliberative and reflective nature of online political activities. For Holmes, one problem with the Internet is the low level of recognition displayed by participants: "the anonymity of the process is exciting because a worldly connection can be made with unknown others, while no responsibility has to be taken for its consequences" (1997, 37). This technology, along with its cohorts—broadcast and virtual reality—possesses solipsistic tendencies; it no longer requires to the same degree social interactions in physical space. Indeed, engagement with the physical world is displaced by a dominant screen culture, which over time becomes the familiar reference point of everyday life.

Holmes's analysis is extremely pessimistic concerning the prospects for an online public sphere contributing to the invigoration of civil society. Indeed, one of the more troubling issues of cyberspace politics is its relationship to real-world practice. Will virtual debates and discussions percolate the political agendas and choices effected in traditional decision-making channels, or will they remain sealed or even vicarious simulations of the real thing? As John Streck puts it, "there seems to be the built-in implication that . . . democracy in cyberspace means democracy in the world" (1998, 40). Streck believes that the issues raised in cyberspace are generally nonissues to those outside. While this is partly an empirical question (one for which Streck provides little evidence), the issue of efficacy also relates to the idea that a person changing channels on television and clicking hypertext on the World Wide Web might mistake these activities for trenchant political action. Volgy and Schwarz (1983) identify a correlation between persons' degrees of exposure to television viewing and vicarious political involvement, a phenomenon that may also characterize browsing the Internet as a stand-in on the part of citizens for actual political participation.

Several alterations can be implemented fairly readily that can potentially ameliorate these liabilities, in both the design and the norms or etiquette of cyberspace. Online political engagement can benefit from the art of conflict resolution, particularly the application of some of the tenets of conflict mediation to cyberspace. Mediation is, put simply, an informal process whereby two or more parties sit down with an independent third person, known as a moderator, who acts as a facilitator to help the parties focus on the issues and to offer reasonable and acceptable solutions or compromises amenable to both or all sides. Figure 7.3 illustrates how this process might take place, with the presentation of information and conferencing being offered so that parties can agree to the overall approach and the issues listed as well as weigh and resolve these issues with the assistance of the facilitator. This process addresses an important pitfall of typical Internet discussions— namely, their unreflective and unresponsive tendencies. By facilitating debates and discussions, issues are crystallized and organized so that decisions and resolutions can be reached following a reasonable period of issue identification, contestation, prioritization, and distillation. Of course, the results or decisions reached are not the only benefits of this conflict-resolution scheme. Participants ideally come to respect and understand other viewpoints and even change or broaden their minds through persuasive argumentation and presentation of information and positions of which the interlocutor was perhaps previously unaware. There are many examples of the successful adoption of conflict-resolution techniques in media environments—telephone, television, and the Internet included—that bode well for the future enhancement of civil online political activity (Becker 1993, 1981; Elgin 1993; Weeks et al. 1992).

The facilitation or moderation of online political forums is critical to their success as agents of decision making or as amplifying issues to be addressed by policy makers. In building bridges—whether it be resolving conflicts, planning neighborhood futures, collaborative problem solving, or prioritizing issues—a skilled and trusted facilitator is often necessary to manage the forum and to create order out of potential chaos (Davis 1999; Dutton 1999). Through the use of widely available software resources, including many web-based programs, a moderator may be able to structure a political forum along the lines presented in figure 7.3.

The proper facilitation of online political discussion, where appropriate, is related to weaving a right to reply into the fabric of conversation and to negotiating difference. A right of response allows participants to exercise a reply to opinions raised in a public forum, particularly those that would add a new facet to the prism of public opinion. I am not suggesting that in all discussions one ought to feel compelled to respond to all messages or points of view. Rather, there should be sufficient reciprocity so that elements of the public do not feel cheated, shoved to the margins, or slighted in any public discussion. This principle ought not to be rigidly adhered to, given the multitude of postings to many forums, but rather should be an informal rule of thumb that becomes part of the etiquette of Internet culture. Procedures similar to the right of reply, such as equal-time and fairness provisions, have been chipped away in recent years under the assumption that diversity of sources via cable and the Internet permit everybody who is potentially affected by an issue to voice her opinion. The Internet is supposedly the most democratic of communicative technologies in allowing any person with access to the medium to respond to a post at any time. However, there is really no responsibility to reply, since messages are addressed to nobody in particular. On many Usenet forums, as was discovered in chapter 5, political debate is frontloaded, with most messages in a forum supportive of a particular candidate or position, which usually means that, over time, the forum will become even more homogeneous, all things being equal. A right of reply would help ensure that different voices are heard, alternative positions are put forward, and no slight or slur is unrequited.

Related to the right of reply as an informal procedure, courtesy, or code of conduct animating the ethos of online civic and political engagement is the need for interforum dialogue so that the balkanization of difference and the customization of culture do not further contribute to the unraveling of American political life. A right of reply fosters respect

**DEMOCRACY IN THE DIGITAL AGE**

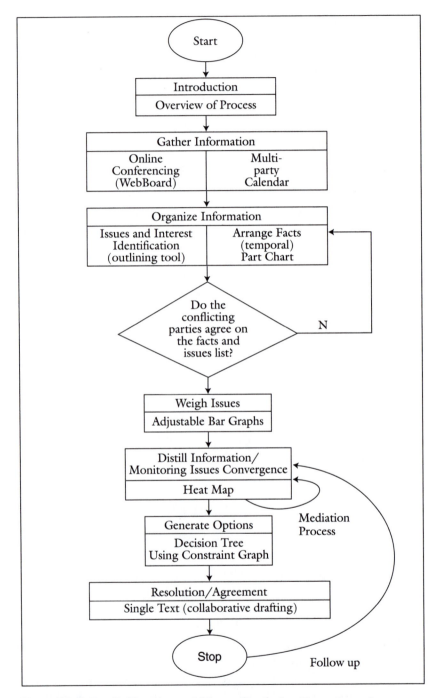

Figure 7.3 Online Deliberation and Dispute Resolution (*Source:* Center for Information Technology and Dispute Resolution 1999)

and responsibility in online discussions while stimulating exchanges between forum participants, particularly those with divergent orientations on issues and candidates. It would benefit the culture and practice of politics online. The niche culture, in which persons scanning online gathering places are likely to form attachments with like-minded individuals, may be comforting and satisfying to the prospective initiate. However, on the level of democratic practice, civic engagement, and social-capital formation, parochial and often intolerant forums ought to be mollified, to the extent possible, with sobering viewpoints from other forums, carried out in good faith, with respect, civility, and goodwill (Carter 1999).

These activities represent several ways in which the solipsistic tendencies of the "screen culture" can be mollified before online forums resemble ideological hornet's nests, to be approached by the "other" at her own risk. If public opinion is going to be more than the sum of superficial, unreflective preferences or the entrenched viewpoint of enclaves of difference, then deliberative and ecumenical exchanges are critical to jostle the minds of the orthodox, to light a fire under the apathetic, and to value the contributions of the subaltern. A well-trained and committed facilitator, participating in forums in which the norm of civility has been inculcated, can elicit these desirable ends and craft a salutary political exchange in which participants come to respect each other and their differences.

## Political Multicasting: An Enduring Public Trusteeship

As broadcasters gear up to provide digital television, much of the buzz surrounding its rollout focuses on the sharper, more lifelike images that dance across the rectangular, high-definition screen. Indeed, the broadcast and electronics industries are banking on newfangled products and services to continue to attract the mass audience to a new and improved screen culture. With an ever-shrinking market share and a distracted, media-soused public, broadcasters' increased spectrum is like the genie let out of the bottle, granting the industry its signal wish—to return television viewership to its golden age.

The problem with this wish is that it may represent the interests of the broadcasters, but the public interest is largely ignored. What are the specific public interests, for example, that merit provision of new spectrum frequencies to incumbent broadcasters for free? Are demands for relevant news content, local programming, and educational content more effectively met via digital service delivery? While privately, over the course of the last decade, broadcasters have been promoting digital television, they have never asked the public what they want and how digital television can best meet their diverse educational, civic, and social needs. Title II of the Telecommunications Act of 1996 states clearly that broadcasters must continue to serve the public interest, convenience, and necessity (§336[d]), which means that broadcasters' obligations must be clearly and specifically enumerated and audited by a vigilant public.

In a pluralistic society, the information needs of residents will vary tremendously. Thus, it is critical that public-interest obligations reflect this diversity rather than take the form of blanket, bland programming that tends to reify existing power relations and endorse the status quo. Peter Dahlgren captures the heart of public-service broadcasting when he says that "not only should all citizens have access to such broadcasting, but the programming should, as far as possible, be aimed at everyone, in the sense of striving to address the needs and interests of the many different groups which comprise society" (1998, 7). This pluralistic vision of society, as one consisting of a multiplicity of groups and public spaces, provides a challenge to public and commercial broadcasting to create formats and to carve out noncommercial channel capacity geared toward meeting these needs rather than simply aggrandizing market share.

While broadcasters might protest that the days of spectrum scarcity are over, given the proliferation of cable television and the Internet, there are at least three reasons to uphold robust public-interest obligations for commercial broadcasters. First, millions of Americans rely on free, over-the-air television for news, information, and educational fare. Cable television is not affordable for many households. Second, the dominant model of Internet service is beginning to resemble the broadcast model, aimed at aggregating and attracting viewership to key online sites in order to please advertisers. The growing commercialization of the Internet means that edifying local and educational materials are buried under advertising banners, a reality particularly troubling for our children (Armstrong and Casement 1998; Healy 1998). Finally, with the cable industry, particularly AT&T, going to a closed architecture (Werbach 1999), limiting content choices for subscribers, it is imperative that regulators provide some venues where the public-interest standard still prevails.

The character of society at any given time is interwoven with the sort of public service that the primary media of the day offer (Grossman 1995). As far back as the debate over the establishment of the American Constitution, there was little disagreement over justifying a free press; rather, the controversy settled around whether the freedom of the press ought to be declared, such as in a bill of rights. In a letter of January 20, 1788, a noted Anti-Federalist stated that "a free press is the channel of communication as to mercantile and public affairs; by means of it the people in large countries ascertain each others sentiments; are enabled to unite, and become formidable to those rulers who adopt improper measures" (Federal Farmer [1788] 1985, 86). From these remarks, it is clear that the purpose of the press was to bring people together, to make people living at geographic distance feel that they were part of something larger than what they could see and visit. Also, the press was meant to keep the people vigilant against the encroachment of tyranny. The Anti-Federalist Centinel called a free press "that grand palladium of freedom, and scourge of tyrants" ([1787] 1985, 19), and this notion that the free press existed first and foremost as protector, as the safeguard of republican government, is the very cornerstone of the First Amendment to the Bill of Rights.

In the present day, the political import of the press in particular and information and communications media in general is often lost on our common understanding of the purposes and aims of media, such as broadcast television. Part of the reason for this shift in thinking rests with what Jürgen Habermas calls a transformation of the public sphere from a culture-debating public to a culture-consuming one. Corresponding with the rise of television viewing in the mid-twentieth century, Habermas describes the displacement of a critical reading public by a mass public of culture consumers:

> the new model of convivial discussion among individuals gave way to more or less noncommittal group activities. These too assumed fixed forms of informal sociability, yet they lacked that specific institutional power that had once ensured the interconnectedness of sociable contacts as the substratum of public communication—no public was formed around "group activities." The characteristic relationship of a privacy oriented toward an audience was also no longer present when people went to the movies together, listened to the radio, or watched TV. (1991, 163)

As the news and public-interest issues were shoved to the slumber hours of television formats and as the distinction between fact and fiction was ever more frequently cast aside, the public sphere of the mass media became one in appearance only. A new reality emerged, one more palatable for consumption, that downplayed and denigrated rational-critical argument as a relic of a bygone era, one before biography displaced politics.

Within this rubric, it is not hard to see how the image of broadcast media as the palladium of liberty became distorted. Indeed, a recent Benton Foundation poll (1999) found that 71 percent of American adults do not know that broadcasters get free access to the airwaves; a majority do not know that just a few corporations own most of the broadcast and cable channels; and a near-majority have heard nothing about digital television and its capacity to do more than provide better picture quality. Once people come to understand and appreciate the issues at hand, however, it becomes clear that the public wants more educational content on television and less violence, to protect their children. The public also wants more public-affairs programming and political broadcasting, although the preferences and viewpoints of the public rather than those of candidates ought to take center stage. In being treated so long as the targets of advertisers and political candidates rather than as public actors with social responsibilities and concerns of a political nature, citizen-consumers have largely forgotten the distinction between public relations and effective political activity.

To restore the public sphere to a state of independence from both the government of the day and private interests is unrealistic in light of the dominance of corporate powers over media outlets, particularly in the United States. Habermas has come to see his own project, as articulated in the early 1960s in *Strukturwandel der Öffentlichkeit*, as unattainable, like Tantalus's grapes. Nicholas Garnham (1992) has attempted to apply Habermas's theory of communicative action to contemporary practices of mass public communication in a pluralistic, decentered social order. Garnham suggests that an understudied area of research for cultural studies and media research is the communicative experiences and identities formed around the borders of systems world and lifeworld, clarification of which may help "discover the media for ms and structures most likely to foster the development of citizens, rather than mere consumers" (374). Dahlgren (1998) also embraces this project, demonstrating how television in Sweden has successfully (in his estimation) popularized and simplified politics and news formats, inviting the involvement of citizens in issues that affect their daily lives (4 f.). This sort of media practice need not succumb to the screen culture. Carving out noncommercial broadcast and Internet capacity may be an uphill battle, but it is not impossible. International examples of noncommercial success are plentiful; noncommercial and nonprofit content aggregators, such as the Internet portal OneWorld, U.K., cuts against the grain of commercial accumulation; and the Gore Commission recommendation to set aside a noncommercial broadcast channel in each community is an idea that some commercial broadcasters may just support, since the alternative would be to auction off recaptured spectrum to new commercial competitors.

The current transition to digital television in the United States highlights the ambivalence of a market-driven system toward fulfilling palpable public-service media obligations. While the convergence of media continues and the language of transmission switches to digital frequencies, the potential of this new multimedia, technologically speaking, is formidable. Broadcasters can harness the frequency spectrum to provide multiple channels rather than just one; furnish services complementary of primary audio and moving images, such as video descriptive services and radio reading services for the deaf and blind; enhance the definition of a single channel; and provide datacasting services for schools.

But the question remains for us: What is its role in enhancing the democratic character of civil society? As Peter Dahlgren suggests, "certainly wide screen will be nice for some programming, but the possibility of more frequency space, to be used for more programming, more diversity, more reprises of key programs, less collision between channels, and video archives, is very promising. The civic culture will be best served by this expansion of public service's capacities" (1998, 12). Lawmakers intended the spectrum giveaway as a response to broadcasters who believed digital television would provide viewers a higher-quality over-the-air product. It is conceivable that the networks may use multiple channels to replay hit shows in different time slots or to set up minicable systems within their compressed and digitized spectrum allotment, but reruns of I Love Lucy would be a far cry from public-affairs and educational programming meant to educate and edify a democratic polity (Postman 1993).

Appropriated to bolster public broadcasting and political and educational programming, multicasting—including multicasting for noncommercial use—would more likely bolster the democratic character of civil society. It should be promoted by policy makers on Capitol Hill and at the FCC, and a percentage of broadcasters' gross revenues should be collected to pay for this potentially powerful capacity, particularly the high cost of developing high-quality programming. Robust programming that is relevant, entertaining, and informative on a range of issues of concern to viewers would provide the public the essential information needed to inform opinions. Providing space for airing local issues, arrived at via ascertainment, would also go a long way toward increasing the interest of viewers in political affairs, broadly defined. More than just supporting candidate-centered discourse in which candidates (most likely major-party candidates) could express their viewpoints and platform positions for five minutes each night for thirty days before an election, multicasting noncommercial public-affairs programming, coupled with provocative political forums airing before elections, would ensure that noteworthy and relevant political content serves a vital public interest in equipping citizens and noncitizens alike with the information they need to signal and address issues to be resolved by lawmaking institutions.

# Conclusion: Media Campaigns and the New International

IN A DEMOCRACY, the preferences and needs of individuals ought to be given equal consideration in the formation of new laws and policies. Formal participation—that is, in choosing representatives—as well as informal activities in civil society are the mechanisms by which persons' preferences are translated into political decision making. The American political system has always fallen short of this democratic ideal, since inequality in formal as well as informal political participation has been a staple of political life from the nation's inception. To rectify egregious inequalities in participation, important amendments have been made to the Constitution. The passage of voting-rights legislation, beginning in the 1960s, also conferred full citizenship rights on minority groups. Notwithstanding these changes to the law, not all U.S. residents have taken full advantage of the new opportunities to participate in political life, for a number of reasons.

Social scientists have long pointed toward economic and social differences as important contributors to unequal formal political participation, and undoubtedly the same disparities affect the extent to which persons are involved in civil society. For example, educational attainment is related to participation in the political public sphere, since one's schooling in general impacts a person's ability to speak and write articulately, to adapt to various social settings, and to apply one's background knowledge to various issues of the day. Life circumstances such as holding down a full-time job and having young children as well as one's language preferences and legal status also affect the extent to which an individual will join a political group, contact a public official, or volunteer. Finally, economic determinants play a significant role in political life, since contributions to political campaigns and the ability to acquire key information and communications resources are tied to one's disposable income.

Many of these obstacles are amplified with the introduction into the political process of advanced information technologies and distributed networking. Some scholars have shown a strong correlation between interconnectivity and democratization, suggesting that freedom is fostered as information and communications tools become more prevalent (Kedzie 1997). However, freedom for whom and to what end are questions continually sidestepped as new technologies are adulated wholesale. As the Danish philosopher Søren Kierkegaard suggested, "people hardly ever make use of the freedom which they have, for example, freedom of thought; instead they demand freedom of speech as a compensation" ([1838] 1946, 10). As the relationship between democracy and telecommunications technology is unraveled, Kierkegaard's statement underscores that, depending on what criteria we use to evaluate a technology, we may arrive at wildly disparate assessments of its worth. If the Internet is judged primarily as a tool to enhance information and communications flow, then it will be evaluated positively. If we alloy this steadfast description of events, it becomes apparent that the purposes for which the technologies are put to use and the ability of all residents to access them undercut the oversanguine assessment of those elites who lack peripheral vision.

Growing inequalities in U.S. society due to asymmetric ownership of advanced telecommunications services (what I am calling the "Red Queen effect") translates into those persons who can access and use the Internet to locate valuable information, exchange ideas, and engage in e-commerce being proportionately better off than those who cannot or will not appropriate these tools. If the worst-off in society do not have the present-day means to express their needs and preferences and if decision makers continue to lavish attention primarily on those corporations and private individuals who can make the largest campaign contributions, then democracy is imperiled.

The evidence for the Red Queen effect and pugnacious immunity to progress among the underprivileged in U.S. society is formidable. A significant portion of the population has never used a computer and currently views computer networks and the Internet as irrelevant to their daily struggles (U. S. Department of Commerce, 1999). While scholars, industry leaders, and the popularizers of the virtual life insinuate that the online world is beginning to resemble America in its demographic makeup, nothing could be farther from the truth. Whereas in 1993 middle-class and affluent households (total annual family income $50,000 and above) with computers comprised 46 percent of all computer owners, the figure in 1998 was 54 percent. Moreover, the poorest households—those with annual family income below $10,000—have slipped from 4 percent of all computer owners in 1993 to 3 percent in 1998. These socioeconomic factors translate into industry neglect of poor communities due to their lack of purchasing power, a reality that, in the absence of government and third-sector assistance, leads to cumulative disadvantage for the worst-off American residents.

This seeming impasse is not easily traversed in a society that is slouching toward full reliance on the private sector to solve entrenched social problems. While each experiment in privatization should be judged in terms of its effectiveness, the momentum has shifted so far toward reliance on the private sector that the public sector appears impotent. Private-sector investment in telecommunications infrastructure deployment in the largest metropolitan areas, such as fiber-optic networks built by competitive local exchange carriers, follows clear patterns of bypassing poor neighborhoods and communities of color in order to maximize profits. More ubiquitous advanced services that upgrade the copper loop, such as digital subscriber lines, are largely unaffordable and unavailable for a significant portion of American residents.

The great economist Adam Smith is known primarily as the father of capitalism; yet he viewed the development of public works and public institutions largely as the responsibility of the commonwealth. For Smith, many public works, such as certain communications and transportation infrastructures, may be clearly advantageous to "a great society" ([1776] 1993; 413); yet they may not be built if the profit cannot be expected to repay the expense to what we call today the private sector. Adam Smith believed that in these circumstances these public works and institutions were to be constructed and their costs defrayed "by the general contribution of the whole society" (443). Several of the projects that Smith highlighted as worthy of public support included "maintaining good roads and communications" as well as "institutions for education." Today, rather than outlining the noble goals of a great society and developing publicly funded programs to meet these goals, we have settled for many private-sector solutions and are content to accept the fallout when the private sector serves only those customers from whom they can expect a reasonable return on their investment. Under these circumstances, Smith advocated a solution—a public solution—whose logic has been turned on its head. If the private sector now and in the future will determine the parameters of a great society, then American society will be limited by the inequalities and gaps in the development of human and material infrastructure that such a system inevitably engenders.

The marketplace juggernaut reflects values and ideals virtually built into the American experience. Beginning around the early to mid-nineteenth century, as Charles Sellars (1991) explains in his brilliant analysis of Jacksonian America, capitalism and markets took on a familiar, modern expression. When Abraham Lincoln was on the stump in the mid-nineteenth century, his rhetoric already reflected that of the modern Prometheus. In his "Lecture on Discoveries and Inventions" of February 11, 1859, Lincoln describes "Young America," a personification of the drive toward globalization, territorial and cultural annexation, self-reliance, and a thirst for novelty. Many of the characteristics of Young America ought to be familiar to us, since they resonate today much as they did during this earlier epoch in American history. Describing Young America as worldwide, Lincoln suggests that American inventiveness and energy would soon sweep the globe. The penchant for the new, coupled with the experimental vein in which improvements are sought for all devices and technologies, echoes today's discussions over the "creative destruction" wrought by the marketplace, evidenced in the ephemeral product cycles of computer and telecommunications devices.

Lincoln goes on in the "Lecture" to link technological advance in important ways with a democratic society and self-governance. Suggesting that invention and innovation derive from "joint operations," such as our "inclination to exchange thoughts with one another" ([1859] 1989, 5), Lincoln links the field of discovery with a democratic vision of progress. The inventions of writing and printing, for example, were sea-change events for Lincoln, because improvements followed rapidly as a greater number of persons were brought into the field of discovery, reflection, inspiration, and experiment. In a wonderful Enlightenment vision, Lincoln says that the outcome of these transformations will be the enhancement of human minds as much as their machines:

> The effects could not come, all at once. It required time to bring them out; and they are still coming. The *capacity* to read, could not be multiplied as fast as the *means* of reading. Spelling-books just began to go into the hands of children; but the teachers were not very numerous, or very competent; so that it is safe to infer they did not advance so speedily as they do now-a-days. It is very probably—almost certain—that the great mass of men, at that time, were utterly unconscious, that their *conditions*, or their *minds* were capable of improvement. ([1859] 1989, 10)

Such a statement could be excerpted from today's headlines as society invests in the new messianic technology, the computer—in classrooms, city halls, and living rooms—with the hope that these implements will facilitate the advancement of society.

While there is much to admire in Lincoln's hopeful paean to human progress—particularly the salutary inventions and ingenious governmental structures put to work in America—the vision strikes one as flawed for several reasons. First, Young America embodies a modern-day Prometheus, who will annex land, create new inventions, and expand knowledge without too much attention to the consequences, intended or otherwise. Lincoln's "Lecture" states unequivocally that the means of information diffusion outpaces the capacity of our institutions to equip citizens for the purpose of navigating a "technological society"; however, it is precisely the collection of talents—not technologies—that determines the quality and direction of republican government. Lincoln's remark certainly resonates in our day as the diffusion of new information and communications technologies reflects the hubris of those promoting "high technology" without attending to the prerequisites of participation in social and political life.

Another flaw in the modern Promethean vision is its disregard for difference. Manifold voices enrich and ennoble democracy, as John Stuart Mill so eloquently put it in his essay, *On Liberty*. If these voices are silenced, then democracy suffers. Whether it be the expansion of the railroad or the Internet, the annexing of territory, physical or virtual, in the name of technological progress and efficiency often wipes out diversity. Lincoln says that Young America has "a great passion—a perfect rage—for the 'new' and has horror and loathing for all that is old, particularly 'Old Fogy.'" All of the divisions of the world will be "re-annexed" in the name of freedom, which means that tradition, diversity, and history will be sacrificed on the altar of progress.

The ultimate tragic flaw of Young America is that moral and political problems are viewed increasingly through the prism of technology, which is seen as a prime mover in the resolution of problems that are primarily social and political in nature. When Aristotle defined human beings as uniquely political animals in Book 1 of the *Politics*, he described us not principally as tool makers and tool users but as political creatures, *zōon politikon*, whose lives in common are meant to sustain good ways of life. If we measure progress by our technological implements, then we are on our way toward believing what the lords of the global village say, that this is the best of all possible worlds. All we need do is improve our implements and the mystery of democracy, as it has been practiced over the past two millennia, will be unveiled. If we provide e-mail to all, then democracy will be made transparent—so say the neofuturists. The clash of values, desires, preferences, and visions of the good life that constitutes politics, however, is never transparent and can never be made so with technology. The opacity and messiness of politics prevents an easy resolution of differences by technological means. As the British philosopher Sir Isaiah Berlin suggests, "the world that we encounter in ordinary experience is one in which we are faced with choices between ends equally ultimate, and claims equally absolute, the realization of some of which must inevitably involve the sacrifice of others" (1969, 168). Since the world in this vision amounts to a contestation of visions of the good life that are often mutually incompatible, negotiation and civility become cardinal virtues, providing the conditions for democratic discussion and deliberation by which citizens' diverse perspectives can be compromised. New technologies, if properly used, can enhance the process by which diverse choices are contested and negotiated; however, to think they can harmonize diverse perspectives would be naive and misguided, like reading *Hamlet* as a comedy. Instead, what is needed, as figure 8.1 highlights, is a clarification of the goals of democracy in the digital age, new perspectives on alternative futures, and bold experimentation with new sociopolitical mechanisms to bring these aspirations closer to realization.

Figure 8.1 illustrates a two-tiered process by which the values and policy goals associated with cyberdemocracy can be brought to fruition. By *cyberdemocracy*, I have meant in this book a more democratic and just social order in which information and communications technologies are deployed to facilitate the fulfillment of democratic values (equity, access, and diversity, just to name a few) in the social practices of everyday life. These democratic values have a normative content that transcends appeals to public-opinion polls and the individual preferences of isolated individuals who are asked to choose from a menu of preselected options developed and cued by accumulated economic and media interests. I take the ideals of a new sociopolitical movement supportive of cyberdemocratic objectives to promote equality, human dignity, and international and intergenerational justice as well as other strong public-interest objectives.

Jacques Derrida's conception of the New International is an appealing one, a sketch of a normative ideal for a new sociopolitical movement that may herald the emigration of new ideas, values, and concepts vis-à-vis telecommunications and media reform to a critical mass of American residents. For Derrida, the New International constitutes "the friendship of an alliance without institutions" (1994, 86), meaning informal movements, free from the interference of governmental and corporate interests, and thus subversive of the status quo. The New International, loosely affiliated or confederated partners, joined by a common set of ideals and values, includes organizations and entities opposed to the untrammeled laws of the marketplace as a surrogate for the public interest. The New International refuses to rest content with liberal

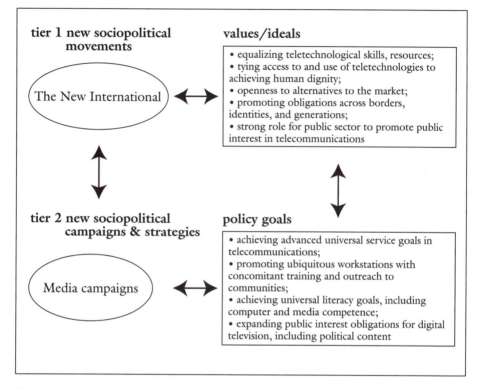

Figure 8.1 Toward Democracy in the Digital Age: A Two-Tiered Approach

democracy's "end-of-history" mantra à la Francis Fukuyama (1992). Its "untimely link" is made among those groups wishing to, among other things, moderate the inequality of technical, scientific, military, and economic development as well as the destruction of the environment and of the "animal life" on the planet.

This sociopolitical movement does not amount to a repudiation of liberal democratic principles; on the contrary, it allies itself with the best they have to offer, an indissoluble link with democracy, justice, and reform principles. Our latest communications marvels, if designed and used wisely, can be allies in the "profound transformation" of the New International as it attempts to pry us loose from our smug end-of-history eschatology and nudge us back into the sanguine political affairs of the day, particularly their redefinition and rethinking across borders, identities, cultures, and levels of economic and technological development. Our task, across difference, is to preserve the earth for future generations, and the question for us becomes whether our governmental and media institutions on the whole promote or hinder this task.

In our openness to a New International there is a call to critique existing practices and for responsibility beyond borders and across time. As Derrida puts it, "to break with the 'party form' or with some form of the State or the International does not mean to give up every form of practical or effective organization. It is exactly the contrary that matters to us here" (1994, 89). A New International thus does more than call into question the ability of entrenched political parties to address the inequalities and injustices rampant on a global scale as well as the capability of ordinary people to amplify their concerns and preferences via channels of communication increasingly owned by a handful of multinational conglomerates. It also has a broader objective than subverting actions by state and international institutions that enhance the well-being of those persons already enjoying affluence while burying the concerns of the preponderance of the world's population under reams of mass-media propaganda. The New International as a counterfactual seeks new forms of practical, democratic organization, in part using the communications technologies at hand as harbingers of these nascent forms of praxis.

New information and communications technologies can facilitate the growth of a New International, particularly given its geographic reach and institutional disaffiliation. A New International as sociopolitical movement can pierce the hegemony of corporate and state monopolies over digital modes of communication, putting them to use to serve the sometimes clandestine and always disestablishment propensities of its supporters. With its global networks able to link citizens supportive of some or all of the tenets of cyberdemocracy—equalizing resources, an openness to alternatives to the market, and so on—a New International bypasses entrenched state and international actors. A reinvigorated civil society can critique and disaffiliate, creating support for new social and political campaigns. One important component of parallel institutions would be inclusive, deliberative, and thus responsible virtual political public spheres, existing to supplement and support a concourse of political activity in the nonvirtual world.

Digitally mediated political life offers little hope of delivering easy or seamless answers to address entrenched problems on a global scale. The ceaseless exchange of high-speed information and the proliferation of political forums demand more of the global citizen, not less. These developments command, among other things, greater critical reflection on the credibility and usefulness of the information being disseminated as well as

greater responsibility in developing solutions to political and social problems that through mainstream venues may remain neglected or ignored.
This should not be confused with the nostrums of futurists who equate
the new with the better. Rather, an acceptance of the new ought to be
evaluated in terms of what it can do to enhance and expedite public-interest values as well as specific public-policy campaigns meant to actualize a
more democratic and egalitarian society.

In his book *Achieving Our Country* (1998), Richard Rorty makes an
important distinction between campaigns and movements that I think is a
helpful one in thinking about how to reform entrenched media and
telecommunications systems. While Derrida's New International vision
provides a normative framework in which to critique existing practice
while positioning ourselves to address the impasses of the current system,
Rorty suggests that we might want to focus on more finite, specific goals
in order to reform the system under which we live. Rather than aligning
ourselves with vast movements that are too big and too amorphous to
succeed in accomplishing anything simple and straightforward, it might
behoove us to set our sights on specific, tangible campaigns. In this way,
alternative public spheres can coalesce around straightforward agendas
and possible solutions that policy makers could propose as new laws. Such
aims as revised universal-service goals, greater attention to public workstations and the human capital to support them, rethinking universal
literacy in the age of the microcomputer, carving out noncommercial
space in digital broadcasting, and linking global citizenship with telecommunications reform constitute salutary media campaigns in the near term.

As is clear from figure 8.1, I suggest that a two-tiered approach to
achieving new political and social objectives related to cyberdemocratic
goals may be more salutary than the either-or picture painted by Rorty.
The counterfactual or normative ideal of the New International provides
a framework in which to rethink and reconceptualize our values and ideas
while simultaneously working politically to effect tangible policy outcomes. In order to impact the policy agenda, the public (and policy
makers as the stewards of the people) needs to influence and cajole others, to persuade them that information and communications technology
issues are as important as jobs, education, economic development, and
political reform. Indeed, reform on the media front—in terms of universal service, public-broadcasting trusteeship, more diverse ownership of
media outlets, and so forth—impinges on these other issues in fundamental ways. While a media reform movement along the lines of a New
International would slowly seep into ordinary people's daily conversations (just as, say, environmental thinking or the rights of homosexuals

are becoming mainstream, becoming "norms"), new media campaigns would push tirelessly for specific reform efforts.

The centrality of telecommunications and new media to all spheres of life precipitates a call to articulate a common interest around which a new international movement and discrete media campaigns can coalesce. Today, evidence of formative common agendas abound, in the growing independent sector and in new community-based and nonprofit collaborations that forge affinities with sister organizations worldwide. Such a constellation of forces is significant but is dimmed by private interests, looming large, at crosspurposes with the long-term public good. Jean-Jacques Rousseau suggests, in his discussion of democracy in the *Social Contract*, that "nothing is more dangerous than the influence of private interests on public affairs" ([1762] 1997, 71). Such a statement may ring hollow today when private interests seem to dominate the political landscape; however, if we look closely we can see the outlines of a countermovement afoot, one that challenges the dominance of the market in our common life.

Control and ownership of the slender glass filaments and coaxial cables through which our ideas and aspirations travel at the speed of light will partly determine our ability to articulate a common voice in virtual (public) spaces. A new activism and experimentation with the technology will be pivotal, but it is conceivable that there will be too many banner advertisements and artful diversions online to maintain our identity as citizens and not just as consumers or Internet travelers. Countervailing publics at that point will speak in different voices and dream different dreams. To weave an alternative narrative to the market-saturated one in the years to come will take concerted leadership in articulating what public right-of-way, ownership, and access to telecommunications and new media technology signify to people's everyday struggles and identities. Moreover, carving out a movement that ties telecommunications reform to an alternative vision for the future will rekindle our wonder at what is possible, a passion that goes to the very heart of what it means to be human.

# APPENDIX A1
## LOGISTIC REGRESSION ANALYSIS OF HOME COMPUTER OWNERSHIP

| Variable† | Logistic Coefficient | Standard Error | Exp (B) |
|---|---|---|---|
| Educate | .1864*** | .0065 | 1.2061 |
| Ethnic (1) | .4093*** | .0673 | 1.5057 |
| Sex (1) | .3447*** | .0317 | 1.4115 |
| Income | .0216*** | .0006 | 1.0218 |
| Job | | | |
|   Job (1) | .3461*** | .0800 | 1.4392 |
|   Job (2) | -.0900 | .0902 | .9139 |
|   Job (3) | -.0659 | .0807 | .9362 |
| Race | | | |
|   Race (1) | .1630 | .1487 | 1.1771 |
|   Race (2) | -.5113* | .1575 | .5997 |
|   Race (3) | -.0294 | .2086 | .9710 |
|   Race (4) | .2872 | .1665 | 1.3327 |
| Constant | -5.2612*** | .1822 | |
| Number of Cases | 33100 | | |
| −2 × log Likelihood Ratio | 41809.241*** | | |
| Percent Correctly Classified | 72.91 | | |

**NOTES**

  \* significant at .05 (one-tailed test)
  \*\* significant at .01 (one-tailed test)
\*\*\* significant at .001 (one-tailed test)

†*Educate*: educational attainment in years / *Ethnic*: 0=Hispanic; 1=non-Hispanic / *Sex*: 0=female; 1=male / *Income*: family income in thousands / *Job*: 1=manager, professional; 2=service; 3=agriculture; 4=manufacturing / *Race*: 1=White; 2=Black; 3=Asian; 4=Native American; 5=other.

*Source*: November 1994 Current Population Survey

# APPENDIX A2
## LOGISTIC REGRESSION ANALYSIS OF HOME MODEM OWNERSHIP

| Variable† | Logistic Coefficient | Standard Error | Exp (B) |
|---|---|---|---|
| Educate | .0566*** | .0094 | 1.0582 |
| Ethnic (1) | .0538 | .1155 | 1.0552 |
| Sex (1) | .2383*** | .0493 | 1.2692 |
| Income | .0074*** | .0009 | 1.0074 |
| Job | | | |
| Job (1) | .7037*** | .1458 | 2.0212 |
| Job (2) | .5073** | .1660 | 1.6607 |
| Job (3) | .3533* | .1495 | 1.4237 |
| Race | | | |
| Race (1) | .4061 | .2542 | 1.5010 |
| Race (2) | .3029 | .2701 | 1.3538 |
| Race (3) | .2347 | .3629 | 1.2645 |
| Race (4) | .2528 | .2740 | 1.2876 |
| Constant | -2.6503*** | .3191 | |
| Number of Cases | 10728 | | |
| −2 × log Likelihood Ratio | 14809.734*** | | |
| Percent Correctly Classified | 57.90 | | |

**NOTES**
   * significant at .05 (one-tailed test)
  ** significant at .01 (one-tailed test)
 *** significant at .001 (one-tailed test)

†*Educate*: educational attainment in years / *Ethnic*: 0=Hispanic; 1=non-Hispanic / *Sex*: 0=female; 1=male / *Income*: family income in thousands / *Job*: 1=manager, professional; 2=service; 3=agriculture; 4=manufacturing / *Race*: 1=White; 2=Black; 3=Asian; 4=Native American; 5=other.

*Source*: November 1994 Current Population Survey

# APPENDIX A3
## LOGISTIC REGRESSION ANALYSIS OF DIGITALLY MEDIATED POLITICAL ENGAGEMENT

| Variable† | Logistic Coefficient | Standard Error | Exp (B) |
|---|---|---|---|
| **Home Network Use** | | | |
| Educate | .1154*** | .0149 | 1.1224 |
| Income | -.0073*** | .0014 | .9927 |
| N=4914 | Percent Correctly Classified: 68.58 | | |
| **Access Government Information** | | | |
| Educate | .1660*** | .0212 | 1.1805 |
| Income | -.0382** | .2417 | .9625 |
| Sex (1) | .2035* | .1008 | 1.2257 |
| N=4904 | Percent Correctly Classified: 83.67 | | |
| **Electronic Voting ("Teledemocracy")** | | | |
| Educate | .0399*** | .0092 | 1.0407 |
| Income | .0324*** | .0061 | 1.0330 |
| Ethnic (1) | -.2435* | .0990 | .7838 |
| Job (1) | .5506*** | .1182 | 1.7342 |
| Job (2) | .5378*** | .1344 | 1.7123 |
| Job (3) | .4206*** | .1202 | 1.5229 |
| N=14047 | Percent Correctly Classified: 68.41 | | |

## NOTES
  * significant at .05 (one-tailed test)
  ** significant at .01 (one-tailed test)
  *** significant at .001 (one-tailed test)

†*Educate*: educational attainment in years / *Ethnic*: 0=Hispanic; 1=non-Hispanic / *Sex*: 0=female; 1=male / *Income*: family income in thousands / *Job*: 1=manager, professional; 2=service; 3=agriculture; 4=manufacturing / *Race*: 1=White; 2=Black; 3=Asian; 4=Native American; 5=other.

*Source*: November 1994 Current Population Survey

# APPENDIX B
# LIST OF (SELF-IDENTIFIED) POLITICAL USENET
# AND AOL FORUMS

*"x" indicates forums randomly chosen
for content analysis*

## Usenet Political Newsgroups

alt.politics.black.helicopters
alt.politics.british
alt.politics.bush
alt.politics.clinton
alt.politics.correct
alt.politics.corruption.mena
alt.politics.datahighway
alt.politics.democrats.d
alt.politics.ec
alt.politics.economics
x-alt.politics.elections
alt.politics.equality
alt.politics.europe.misc
alt.politics.greens
alt.politics.homosexuality
alt.politics.immigration
alt.politics.italy
alt.politics.korea
x-alt.politics.libertarian
x-alt.politics.media
alt.politics.meijer
alt.politics.nationalism.black
alt.politics.nationalism.white
alt.politics.org.batf
x-alt.politics.org.cia
alt.politics.org.fbi
alt.politics.org.misc
alt.politics.org.nsa
alt.politics.org.un
alt.politics.perot
alt.politics.radical-left
x-alt.politics.reform
alt.suburbs
alt.politics.sex
alt.politics.socialism.mao

alt.politics.socialism.trotsky
alt.politics.usa.congress
alt.politics.usa.constitution
alt.politics.usa.misc
alt.politics.usa.newt-gingrich
alt.politics.usa.republican
alt.politics.vietnamese
x-alt.politics.white-power
alt.politics.youth
talk.politics.animals
talk.politics.china
talk.politics.crypto
talk.politics.drugs
talk.politics.european-union
talk.politics.guns
talk.politics.libertarian
talk.politics.medicine
talk.politics.mideast
talk.politics.misc
talk.politics.soviet
talk.politics.theory
talk.politics.tibet

## AOL's Washington Connection

x-Abortion
x-Decision 96
Domestic Issues
Federal Budget and Taxes
The Fence Post
Forum Feedback
General Debate
Gun Control
Immigration
International Issues
Pending Legislation
x-Political Viewpoint
x-Welfare
White House

# REFERENCES

Advisory Committee on Public Interest Obligations of Digital Television Broadcasters (PIAC). 1998. *Charting the Digital Broadcasting Future.* Washington, D.C. Available: www.benton.org/PIAC.

Alliance for Public Technology. 1998a. *Petition of the Alliance for Public Technology Requesting Issuance of Notice of Inquiry and Notice of Proposed Rulemaking to Implement Section 706 of the 1996 Telecommunications Act.* Washington, D.C.: Alliance for Public Technology.

———. 1998b. *Blueprints for Action: New Strategies for Achieving Universal Service.* Washington, D.C.: Alliance for Public Technology.

American Civil Liberties Union et al. 1996. "Appellee Brief in *Reno v. ACLU,*" no. 96–511. Available: http://www.aclu.org/court/renovaclu.html.

Anderson, Robert H., Tora K. Bikson, Sally Ann Law, and Bridger M. Mitchell. 1995. *Universal Access to E-mail: Feasibility and Societal Implications.* Santa Monica, Calif.: RAND.

Arendt, Hannah. 1977. *Between Past and Future.* New York: Penguin.

———. 1973. *The Origins of Totalitarianism.* San Diego: Harvest.

———. 1958. *The Human Condition.* Chicago: University of Chicago Press.

Armstrong, Alison, and Charles Casement. 1998. *The Child and the Machine: Why Computers May Put Our Children's Education at Risk.* Toronto: Key Porter.

Arterton, F. Christopher. 1987. *Teledemocracy: Can Technology Protect Democracy?* Newbury Park: Sage.

Aspen Institute. 1999. *Residential Access to Bandwidth: Exploring New Paradigms.* Washington, D.C.: The Aspen Institute.

Aufderheide, Patricia. 1999. *Communications Policy and the Public Interest.* New York: Guilford.

Aurigi, Alessandro, and Stephen Graham. 1998. "The 'Crisis' in the Urban Public Realm." In *Cyberspace Divide: Equality, Agency and Policy in the Information Society,* edited by Brian D. Loader, 57–80. London: Routledge.

Bagdikian, Ben H. 1997. *The Media Monopoly,* 5th ed. Boston: Beacon.

Barber, Benjamin R. 1998. *A Passion for Democracy: American Essays.* Princeton, N.J.: Princeton University Press.

———. 1995. *Jihad vs. McWorld.* New York: Times Books.

**REFERENCES**

———. 1984. *Strong Democracy: Participatory Politics for a New Age*. Berkeley: University of California Press.

Barker, Michael, and Randy Barber. 1998. *The Coup of the Century? Another Look at the MCI-WorldCom Merger*. Washington, D.C.: Communications Workers of America.

Baydar, Nazli, Jeanne Brooks-Gunn, and Frank F. Furstenberg. 1993. "Early Warning Signs of Functional Illiteracy: Predictors in Childhood and Adolescence." *Child Development* 64(3): 815–29.

Becker, Lee B. 1987. "A Decade of Research on Interactive Cable." In *Wired Cities: Shaping the Future of Communications*, edited by William H. Dutton, Jay G. Blumler, and Kenneth L. Kraemer, 102–23. Boston: G. K. Hall & Co.

Becker, Theodore L. 1993. "Teledemocracy: Gathering Momentum in State and Local Governance." *Spectrum: The Journal of State Government* 66(2): 14–19.

———. 1981. "Teledemocracy: Bringing Power Back to the People." *The Futurist* 15(6): 6–9.

Bekkers, V. J. J. M. 1997. "The Emergence of the Electronic Superhighway: Do Politics Matter?" In *The Social Shaping of Information Superhighways: European and American Roads to the Information Society*, edited by Herbert Kubicek, William H. Dutton, and Robin Williams, 157–72. New York: St. Martin's Press.

Belinfante, Alexander. 1998. *Telephone Subscribership in the United States*. Washington, D.C.: Federal Communications Commission.

Benedikt, Michael. 1991. "Cyberspace: Some Proposals." In *Cyberspace: First Steps*, edited by Michael Benedikt, 119–224. Cambridge, Mass.: MIT Press.

Benhabib, Seyla. 1992. "Models of Public Space: Hannah Arendt, the Liberal Tradition, and Jürgen Habermas." In *Habermas and the Public Sphere*, edited by Craig Calhoun, 73–98. Cambridge, Mass.: MIT Press.

Benton Foundation. 1999. "The Debate on the Future of Television." Available: http://www.benton.org/Policy/TV/.

Berlin, Isaiah. 1969. *Four Essays on Liberty*. Oxford: Oxford University Press.

Bernoff, Josh. 1998. Summary of panel presentation from Advisory Committee on Public Interest Obligations of Digital Television Broadcasters. Available: http://www.benton.org/PIAC/.

Bimber, Bruce. 1998a. "Toward an Empirical Mapping of Political Participation on the Internet." Paper presented at the 1998 annual meeting of the American Political Science Association, Boston.

———. 1998b. "The Internet and Citizen Communication with Government: Does the Medium Matter?" Paper presented at the 1998 annual meeting of the American Political Science Association, Boston.

Birdsell, David, Douglas Muzzio, David Krane, and Amy Cottreau. 1998. "Web Users Are Looking More like America." *The Public Perspective*. Available: http://www.ropercenter.uconn.edu/pubper/pp93.htm.

Blackburn, McKinley L., David E. Bloom, and Richard E. Freeman. 1989. *The Declining Economic Position of Less-Skilled American Males*. NBER Working Paper no. 3186. Cambridge, Mass.: National Bureau of Economic Research, Inc.

Blau, Andrew. 1997. "A High Wire Act in a Highly Wired World: Universal Service and the Telecommunications Act of 1996." In *The Social Shaping of*

*Information Superhighways: European and American Roads to the Information Society*, edited by Herbert Kubicek, William H. Dutton, and Robin Williams, 247–63. New York: St. Martin's Press.

Bryan, Cathy, Roza Tsagarousianou, and Damian Tambini. 1998. "Electronic Democracy and the Civic Networking Movement in Context." In *Cyberdemocracy: Technology, Cities, and Civic Networking*, edited by Roza Tsagarousianou, Damian Tambini, and Cathy Bryan, 1–17. London: Routledge.

Budge, Ian. 1996. *The New Challenge of Direct Democracy*. Cambridge: Blackwell.

Burgelman, J.-C. 1994. "Assessing Information Technologies in the Information Society" In *Information Society and Civil Society*, edited by Slavko Splichal, Andrew Calabrese, and Colin Sparks, 185–207. West Lafayette, Ind.: Purdue University Press.

Burke, Edmund. 1987 [1790]. *Reflections on the Revolution in France*. Indianapolis: Hackett.

Canovan, Margaret. 1992. *Hannah Arendt: A Reinterpretation of Her Political Thought*. New York: Cambridge University Press.

Carroll, Lewis. 1960. *Alice's Adventures in Wonderland and Through the Looking-Glass*. New York: Signet Classic.

Carter, Stephen L. 1999. *Civility: Manners, Morals, and the Etiquette of Democracy*. New York: HarperCollins.

Case, Anne C., and Lawrence F. Katz. 1991. *The Company You Keep: The Effects of Family and Neighborhood on Disadvantaged Youth*. NBER Working Paper no. 3705. Cambridge, Mass.: National Bureau of Economic Research, Inc.

Castells, Manuel. 1998. *End of Millennium*. Oxford: Blackwell.

———. 1996. *The Rise of the Network Society*. Oxford: Blackwell.

Center for Information Technology and Dispute Resolution. 1999. "Dispute Resolution Flowchart." Available: http://128.119.199.27/process/.

Center for Media Education. 1998. *Deepening the Digital Divide: The War on Universal Service*. Washington, D.C.: Center for Media Education.

Center for Media Education et al. 1994. *Petition for Relief from Unjust and Unreasonable Discrimination in the Deployment of Video Dialtone Facilities*. Washington, D.C.: Federal Communications Commission.

Centinel. 1985 [1787]. "Letter to the *Independent Gazetteer* and *Freeman's Journal*." In *The Anti-Federalist*, edited by Herbert J. Storing, 7–22. Chicago: University of Chicago Press.

Chen, Milton. 1986. "Gender and Computers: The Beneficial Effects of Experience on Attitudes." *Journal of Educational Computing Research* 293: 265–81.

Chomsky, Noam. 1993. "Media Control." In *Open Fire*, edited by Greg Ruggiero and Stuart Sahulka, 267–90. New York: New Press.

Civille, Richard. 1995. "The Internet and the Poor." In *Public Access to the Internet*, edited by Brian Kahin and James Keller, 175–207. Cambridge, Mass.: MIT Press.

Cohen, Jean L., and Andrew Arato. 1992. *Civil Society and Political Theory*. Cambridge, Mass.: MIT Press.

**REFERENCES**

Commission on Freedom of the Press. 1947. *A Free and Responsible Press: A General Report on Mass Communication*. Chicago: University of Chicago Press.

Connolly, William E. 1995. *The Ethos of Pluralization*. Minneapolis: University of Minnesota Press.

Cooper, Mark. 1998. *Stonewalling Local Competition: The Baby Bell Strategy for Subverting the Telecommunications Act of 1996*. Washington, D.C.: Consumer Federation of America.

———. 1996. *Universal Service: A Historical Perspective and Policies for the Twenty-First Century*. Washington, D.C.: The Consumer Federation of America and the Benton Foundation. Available: http://www.benton.org/Library/Prospects/prospects.html.

Cottrell, Janet. 1992. "I'm a Stranger Here Myself: A Consideration of Women in Computing." *Learning from the Past, Stepping into the Future*. New York: Association of Computing Machinery.

Coupland, Douglas. 1991. *Generation X: Tales for an Accelerated Culture*. New York: St. Martin's Press.

Cronin, Thomas E. 1989. *Direct Democracy: The Politics of Initiative, Referendum and Recall*. Cambridge, Mass.: Harvard University Press.

Dahl, Richard A. 1996. "Equality versus Inequality." *PS: Political Science and Politics* 29(4): 639–48.

———. 1989. *Democracy and Its Critics*. New Haven: Yale University Press.

———. 1970 *After the Revolution: Authority in a Good Society*. New Haven: Yale University Press.

Dahlgren, Peter. 1998. "Public Service Media, Old and New: Vitalizing a Civic Culture?" The 1998 Spry Memorial Lecture. Available: http://www.fas.umontreal.ca/COM/spry/spry-pd-lec.html.

Davis, Richard. 1999. *The Web of Politics: The Internet's Impact on the American Political System*. New York: Oxford University Press.

Dennis, Alan R., and Joseph S. Valacich. 1993. "Computer Brainstorms: More Heads Are Better than One." *Journal of Applied Psychology* 78: 531–37.

Derrida, Jacques. 1994. *Specters of Marx*, translated by Peggy Kamuf. New York: Routledge.

———. 1992. *The Other Heading: Reflections on Today's Europe*, translated by Pascale-Anne Brault and Michael B. Naas. Bloomington: Indiana University Press.

Dewey, John. 1954[1927]. *The Public and Its Problems*. Athens: Ohio University Press.

———. 1966 [1916]. *Democracy and Education*. New York: Free Press.

Docter, Sharon, and William H. Dutton. 1998. "The First Amendment Online: Santa Monica's Public Electronic Network." In *Cyberdemocracy: Technology, Cities and Civic Networks*, edited by Roza Tsagarousianou, Damian Tambini, and Cathy Bryan, 125–51. London: Routledge.

Dole, Robert. 1994. Press release on the Telecommunications Act of 1994, September 23.

Dowmunt, Tony, editor. 1993. *Channels of Resistance: Global Television and Local Empowerment*. London: British Film Institute.

Downs, Anthony. 1957. *An Economic Theory of Democracy*. New York: Harper & Brothers.

Drake, William J. 1995. "The Turning Point." In *The New Information Infrastructure: Strategies for U.S. Policy*, edited by William J. Drake, 1–27. New York: Twentieth Century Fund Press.

Drucker, Peter F. 1993. *Post-Capitalist Society.* New York: HarperBusiness.

Dutton, William H. 1999. *Society on the Line: Information Politics in the Digital Age.* Oxford: Oxford University Press.

———. 1996. "Network Rules of Order: Regulating Speech in Public Electronic Fora." *Media, Culture & Society* 18: 269–90.

———. 1994. "Lessons from Public and Nonprofit Services." In *The People's Right to Know: Media, Democracy and the Information Highway,* edited by Frederick Williams and John V. Pavlik, 105–37. Hillsdale, N.J.: Lawrence Erlbaum Associates.

Dutton, William H., Patrick L. Sweet, and Everett M. Rogers. 1989. "Socioeconomic Status and the Early Diffusion of Personal Computing in the United States." *Social Science Computer Review* 7(3): 259–72.

Dyson, Esther. 1997. *Release 2.0: A Design for Living in the Digital Age.* New York: Broadway Books.

Dyson, Esther, George Gilder, George Keyworth, and Alvin Toffler. 1994. *Cyberspace and the American Dream: A Magna Carta for the Knowledge Age.* Available: http://www.pff.org/position.html.

Economic Policy Institute. 1999. *The State of Working America 1998-99.* Ithaca, N.Y.: Cornell University Press.

Education and Library Networks Coalition (EdLiNC). 1999. *E-Rate: Connecting Kids & Communities to the Future.* Washington, D.C.: EdLiNC.

Elgin, Duane. 1993. "Revitalizing Democracy Through Electronic Town Meetings." *Spectrum: The Journal of State Government* 66(2): 6–13.

Elshtain, Jean Bethke. 1982. "Democracy and the QUBE Tube." *The Nation* 235(4): 108–10.

Farhi, Paul. 1999. "Fears Rise of a 'Digital Divide.'" *The Washington Post,* May 25, E1.

Federal Communications Commission. 1999. *Inquiry Concerning the Deployment of Advanced Telecommunications Capability to All Americans in a Reasonable and Timely Fashion and Possible Steps to Accelerate Such Deployment Pursuant to Section 706 of the Telecommunications Act of 1996.* Washington, D.C.: Federal Communications Commission.

Federal Farmer. 1985 [1788]. "Observations Leading to a Fair Examination of the System of Government Proposed by the Late Convention; and to Several Essential and Necessary Alterations to It." In *The Anti-Federalist,* edited by Herbert J. Storing, 23–101. Chicago: University of Chicago Press.

Fischer, Claude S. 1992. *America Calling: A Social History of the Telephone to 1940.* Berkeley: University of California Press.

Fisher, Allan, Jane Margolis, and Faye Miller. 1997. "Undergradate Women in Computer Science: Experience, Motivation and Culture." Article appeared in proceedings of the *ACM SIGCSE* Technical Symposium.

Fisher, B., M. Margolis, and D. Resnick. 1994. "A New Way of Talking Politics: Democracy on the Internet." Paper presented at the 1994 American Political Science Association annual conference, Washington, D.C.

Fishkin, James S. 1995. *The Voice of the People: Public Opinion and Democracy.* New Haven: Yale University Press.

———. 1992. "Beyond Teledemocracy: 'America on the Line.'" *The Responsive Community* 2(3): 13–19.

———. 1991. *Democracy and Deliberation: New Directions for Democratic Reform.* New Haven: Yale University Press.

**REFERENCES**

Frank, Glenn. 1935. "Radio as an Educational Force." In *Radio: The Fifth Estate*, edited by Herman S. Hettinger, 119–22. Philadelphia: Annals of the American Academy of Political and Social Science.

Friedman, David. 1999. "The Dark Side of the High-Tech Religion." *Los Angeles Times*, January 31, M1.

Fukuyama, Francis. 1992. *The End of History and the Last Man*. New York: Free Press.

Galbraith, John Kenneth. 1958. *The Affluent Society*. Boston: New American Library.

Gardner, J. R., A. McEwen, and C. A. Curry. 1986. "A Sample Survey of Attitudes to Computer Studies." *Computers and Education* 10(2): 293–98.

Garnham, Nicholas. 1992 "The Media and the Public Sphere." In *Habermas and the Public Sphere*, edited by Craig Calhoun, 359–76. Cambridge, Mass.: MIT Press.

———. 1990. *Capitalism and Communication*. London: Sage.

Geertz, Clifford. 1973. *The Interpretation of Cultures*. New York: Basic Books.

Gitlin, Todd. 1993. "Flat and Happy." *The Wilson Quarterly* 17(4): 47–55.

Goldin, Claudia D., and Lawrence F. Katz. 1995. *The Decline of Noncompeting Groups: Changes in the Premium to Education, 1890 to 1940*. NBER Working Paper no. 5202. Cambridge, Mass.: National Bureau of Economic Research, Inc.

Golding, Peter. 1997. "World Wide Wedge: Division and Contradiction in the Global Information Infrastructure." *Monthly Review* 48(3): 70–85.

———. 1990. "Political Communication and Citizenship: The Media and Democracy in an Inegalitarian Social Order." In *Public Communication, The New Imperatives: Future Directions for Media Research*, edited by Marjorie Ferguson, 84–100. London: Sage.

Graphic, Visualization, and Usability Center. 1998. "Seventh World Wide Web User Study." Available: http://www.cc.gatech.edu/gvu/user_surveys/.

Groper, Richard. 1996. "Electronic Mail and the Reinvigoration of American Democracy." *Social Science Computer Review* 14(2): 157–68.

Grossman, Lawrence K. 1995. *The Electronic Republic: The Transformation of American Democracy*. New York: Viking.

Guthrie, K. Kendall, and William H. Dutton. 1992. "The Politics of Citizen Access Technology: The Development of Public Information Utilities in Four Cities." *Policy Studies Journal* 20(4): 574–97.

Habermas, Jürgen. 1996. *Between Facts and Norms: Contributions to a Discourse Theory of Law and Democracy*, translated by William Rehg. Cambridge, Mass.: MIT Press.

———. 1991. *The Structural Transformation of the Public Sphere*, translated by Thomas Burger with Frederick Lawrence. Cambridge, Mass.: MIT Press.

———. 1990. *Moral Consciousness and Communicative Action*, translated by Christian Lenhardt and Shierry Weber Nicholsen. Cambridge, Mass.: MIT Press.

———. 1987. *The Theory of Communicative Action*, vol. 2, *Lifeworld and System: A Critique of Functionalist Reasoning*, translated by Thomas McCarthy. Boston: Beacon Press.

———. 1984. *The Theory of Communicative Action*, vol. 1, *Reason and the Rationalization of Society*, translated by Thomas McCarthy. Boston: Beacon Press.

———. 1983. *Philosophical-Political Profiles*, translated by Frederick Lawrence. Cambridge: MIT Press.

———. 1979. *Communication and the Evolution of Society*, translated by Thomas McCarthy. Boston: Beacon Press.

Hacker, Kenneth L. 1996. "Missing Links in the Evolution of Electronic Democratization." *Media, Culture & Society* 18: 213–32.

Harrington, Michael. 1962. *The Other America: Poverty in the United States*. New York: Penguin.

Healy, Jane M. 1998. *Failure to Connect: How Computers Affect Our Children's Minds—for Better and Worse*. New York: Simon and Schuster.

Heidegger, Martin. 1977 [1952]. "The Question Concerning Technology." In *The Question Concerning Technology and Other Essays*, translated by William Lovitt, 3–35. New York: Harper & Row.

Herring, Susan. 1994. "Gender Differences in Computer-Mediated Communication: Bringing Familiar Baggage to the New Frontier." Paper presented at the American Library Association annual convention, Miami.

Hess, Robert S., and Irene T. Miura. 1985. "Gender Differences in Enrollment in Computer Camps." *Sex Roles* 13(3–4): 165–80.

Hirschkop, Ken. 1996. "Democracy and the New Technologies." *Monthly Review* 48(3): 86–98.

Hoffman, Donna L., and Thomas P. Novak. 1998. "Bridging the Racial Divide on the Internet." *Science* 280: 390–91.

Holderness, Mike, 1998. "Who Are the World's Information-Poor?" In *Cyberspace Divide: Equality, Agency and Policy in the Information Society*, edited by Brian D. Loader, 35–56. London: Routledge.

Holmes, David. 1997. "Virtual Identity: Communities of Broadcast, Communities of Interactivity." In *Virtual Politics: Identity and Community in Cyberspace*, edited by David Holmes, 26–45. London: Sage.

Holub, Robert C. 1991. *Jürgen Habermas: Critic in the Public Sphere*. London: Routledge.

Huckfeldt, Robert R., and John Sprague. 1995. *Citizens, Politics, and Social Communication*. Cambridge, Mass.: Cambridge University Press.

Information Infrastructure Task Force. 1993. *The National Information Infrastructure: Agenda for Action*. Washington, D.C.: National Telecommunications and Information Administration.

Information Superhighway Task Force Report. 1995. City of Phoenix, February 27.

Jakubowicz, Karol. 1994. "Civil Society, Independent Public Sphere, and Information Society." In *Information Society and Civil Society*, edited by Slavko Splichal, Andrew Calabrese, and Colin Sparks, 78–102. West Lafayette, Ind.: Purdue University Press.

Jameson, Fredric. 1991. *Postmodernism, or, the Cultural Logic of Late Capitalism*. Durham, N.C.: Duke University Press.

Janda, Kenneth. 1978. "A Microfilm and Computer System for Analyzing Comparative Politics Literature." In *The Analysis of Communication Content*, edited by George Gerbner et al., 407–35. Huntington, N.Y.: Robert E. Krieger Publishers.

Jefferson, Thomas. 1984 [1787]. "Letter to Edward Carrington." In *Thomas Jefferson: Writings*, edited by Merrill D. Peterson, 879–81. New York: Library of America.

**REFERENCES**

Josephson, Matthew. 1959. *Edison: A Biography*. New York: McGraw-Hill.

Kahn, Frank J., editor. 1973. *Documents of American Broadcasting*. New York: Appleton-Century-Crofts.

Katz, Jon. 1997. "The Digital Citizen," *Wired*. Available: http://www.hotwired.com/special/citizen/.

Kedzie, Christopher R. 1997. "The Third Waves." In *Borders in Cyberspace: Information Policy and the Global Information Infrastructure*, edited by Brian Kahin and Charles Nesson, 106–28. Cambridge, Mass.: MIT Press.

Kellner, Douglas. 1998. "Intellectuals, the New Public Spheres, and Techno-Politics." In *The Politics of Cyberspace*, edited by Chris Toulouse and Timothy W. Luke, 167–86. New York: Routledge.

Kelly, Caroline. 1989. "Political Identity and Perceived Intragroup Homogeneity." *British Journal of Social Psychology* 28(3): 239–50.

Kennard, William E. 1998. "Remarks to the International Radio and Television Society." Available: http://www.fcc.gov/Speeches/Kennard/spwek827.htm.

Kierkegaard, Søren. 1946 [1838]. *A Kierkegaard Anthology*, edited by Robert Bretall. Princeton, N. J.: Princeton University Press.

Kiesler, Sara, and Lee S. Sproull. (1992) "Group Decision Making and Communication Technology." *Organizational Behavior and Human Decision Making* 52: 96–123.

Kirby, Michael. 1971. *Futurist Performance*. New York: E. P. Dutton & Co., Inc.

Kozol, Jonathan. 1985. *Illiterate America*. Garden City, N.Y.: Anchor Press.

Krasnow, Erwin G. 1997. *The Public Interest Standard: The Elusive Search for the Holy Grail*. Briefing paper prepared for the Advisory Committee on Public Interest Obligations of Digital Television Broadcasters. Available: http://www.ntia.doc.gov/pubintadvcom/octmtg/krasnow.htm.

Krendl, Kathy A., Mary C. Brohier, and Cynthia Fleetwood. 1989. "Children and Computers: Do Sex-Related Differences Persist?" *Journal of Communication* 39(3): 85–93.

Krippendorff, Klaus. 1980. *Content Analysis: An Introduction to Its Methodologies*. Beverly Hills: Sage.

Lenert, Edward M. 1998. "A Communication Theory Perspective on Telecommunications Policy." *Journal of Communication* 48(4): 3–23.

Lilley, William. 1998. Remarks and Maps Prepared for Aspen Institute Workshop [August 24]. Washington, D.C.: InContext, Inc.

Lincoln, Abraham. 1989 [1859]. "Lecture on Discoveries and Inventions." In *Abraham Lincoln: Speeches and Writings, 1859–1865*, edited by Don E. Fehrenbacher, 3–11. New York: Library of America.

Lloyd, Mark. 1997. Transcript of panel presentation from Advisory Committee on Public Interest Obligations of Digital Television Broadcasters. Available: http://www.benton.org/PIAC.

Loader, Brian D. 1998. "Cyberspace Divide: Equality, Agency and Policy in the Information Society." In *Cyberspace Divide: Equality, Agency and Policy in the Information Society*, edited by Brian D. Loader, 3–16. London: Routledge.

Luke, Timothy W. 1998. "The Politics of Digital Inequality." In *The Politics of Cyberspace*, edited by Chris Toulouse and Timothy W. Luke, 120–43. New York: Routledge.

MacKie-Mason, Jeffrey, and Hal R. Varian. 1995. "Pricing the Internet." In *Public Access to the Internet*, edited by Brian Kahin and James Keller, 269–314. Cambridge, Mass.: MIT Press.

Mann, Thomas. 1938. *The Coming Victory of Democracy*. New York: Alfred A. Knopf.

Marinetti, Filippo Tommaso. 1991 [1909]. *Let's Murder the Moonshine: Selected Writings*, translated by R. W. Flint and Arthur A. Coppotelli. Los Angeles: Sun & Moon Classics.

Marx, Karl, and Friedrich Engels. 1978 [1848]. *Manifesto of the Communist Party*. In *The Marx-Engels Reader*, edited by Robert C. Tucker, 469–500. New York: W. W. Norton.

Mazmanian, Daniel A., Sherry Bebitch Jeffe, and Anthony G. Wilhelm. 1995. *Issues in Telecommunications and Democracy*. Communications Policy Working Paper no. 8. Washington, D.C.: The Benton Foundation.

McChesney, Kristine S. 1998. Telephone interview, October 5.

McChesney. Robert W. 1997a. "The Mythology of Commercial Broadcasting and the Contemporary Crisis of Public Broadcasting." The 1997 Spry Memorial Lecture. Available: http://www.fas.umontreal.ca/COM/spry/spry-rm-lec.html.

———. 1997b. *Corporate Media and the Threat to Democracy*. New York: Seven Stories Press.

———. 1996. "The Internet and U.S. Communication Policy-Making in Historical and Critical Perspective." *Journal of Communication* 46(1): 98–124.

———. 1993. *Telecommunications, Mass Media and Democracy*. New York: Oxford University Press.

McConnaughey, James W. 1997. "Access to the Information Superhighway." In *The Social Shaping of Information Superhighways: European and American Roads to the Information Society*, edited by Herbert Kubicek, William H. Dutton, and Robin Williams, 221–31. New York: St. Martin's Press.

McWilliams, Wilson Carey. 1993. "Science and Freedom: America as the Technological Republic." In *Technology in the Western Political Tradition*, edited by Arthur M. Melzer, Jerry Weinberger, and M. Richard Zinman, 85–108. Ithaca, N.Y.: Cornell University Press.

Medina, Rosa M. 1998. Interview, October 16.

Miller, Steven E. 1996. *Civilizing Cyberspace: Policy, Power and the Information Highway*. New York: ACM.

Monberg, John. 1998. "Making the Public Count: A Comparative Case Study of Emergent Information Technology-Based Publics." *Communication Theory* 8(4): 426–54.

Mosco, Vincent. 1998. "The Socio-Cultural Implications of a Knowledge-Based Society: A Prospective Research Survey." Paper presented to Knowledge-based Economy and Society Pilot Project, Workshop 1, Evidence Concerning the Emergence, Dynamics, and Requirements of the Knowledge-based Economy and Society. International Comparative Research Group, Hull, Quebec.

Mueller, Milton, and Jorge R. Schement. 1995. *Universal Service from the Bottom Up: A Profile of Telecommunications Access in Camden, New Jersey*. Available: http://ba.com/reports/rutgers/ba-title.html.

Murdock, Graham, and Peter Golding. 1989. "Information Poverty and Political Inequality: Citizenship in the Age of Privatized Communications." *Journal of Communication* 39(3): 180–95.

Naisbitt, John. 1982. *Megatrends: Ten New Directions Transforming Our Lives.* New York: Warner Books.

Negroponte, Nicholas. 1995. *Being Digital.* New York: Knopf.

Neu, C. Richard, Robert H. Anderson, and Tora K. Bikson. 1998. *E-mail Communication between Government and Citizens.* Santa Monica, Calif.: RAND.

Neuman, W. Russell. 1991 *The Future of the Mass Audience.* New York: Cambridge University Press.

Petracca, Mark P. 1991. "The Rational Choice Approach to Politics: A Challenge to Democratic Politics." *Review of Politics* 53: 289–319.

Pew Research Center. 1999. "Online Newcomers More Middle-Brow, Less Work-Oriented." Available: http://www.people press.org/tech98sum. htm.

Pool, Ithiel de Sola. 1984. "Competition and Universal Service: Can We Get There from Here?" In *Disconnecting Bell: The Impact of the AT&T Divestiture,* edited by Harry M. Shooshan III, 112–31. New York: Pergamon.

———. 1983. *Technologies of Freedom.* Cambridge, Mass.: Harvard University Press.

Poster, Mark. 1997. "Cyberdemocracy: The Internet and the Public Sphere." In *Virtual Politics: Identity and Community in Cyberspace,* edited by David Holmes, 212–28. London: Sage.

Postman, Neil. 1993. *Technopoly: The Surrender of Culture to Technology.* New York: Vintage.

Raab, Charles, Christine Bellamy, John Taylor, William H. Dutton, and Malcolm Peltu. 1996. "The Information Polity: Electronic Democracy, Privacy, and Surveillance." In *Information and Communication Technologies: Visions and Realities,* edited by William H. Dutton, 283–99. Oxford: Oxford University Press.

Rasmussen, David M. 1990. *Reading Habermas.* Oxford: Basil Blackwell.

Rawls, John. 1993. *Political Liberalism.* New York: Columbia University Press.

Reich, Robert B. 1997. "Sky and Ground." *The New Yorker* 73(26): 7–8.

———. 1991. *The Work of Nations.* New York: Vintage.

Resnick, David. 1998 "Politics on the Internet: The Normalization of Cyberspace." In *The Politics of Cyberspace,* edited by Chris Toulouse and Timothy W. Luke, 48–68. New York: Routledge.

Rheingold, Howard. 1993. *The Virtual Community: Homesteading on the Electronic Frontier.* New York: Addison-Wesley.

Rifkin, Jeremy. 1995. *The End of Work: The Decline of the Global Labor Force and the Dawn of the Post-Market Era.* New York: G. P. Putnam's Sons.

Rogers, Everett M., and D. Lawrence Kincaid. 1981. *Communication Networks: Toward a New Paradigm for Research.* New York: Free Press.

Roosevelt, Franklin D. 1996 [1937]. "Second Inaugural Address." In *The Essential Franklin Delano Roosevelt,* edited by John Gabriel Hunt, 127–40. Avenel, N.J.: Portland House.

Roper, Juliet. 1998. "New Zealand Political Parties Online: The World Wide Web as a Tool for Democratization or for Political Marketing?" In *The Politics of Cyberspace*, edited by Chris Toulouse and Timothy W. Luke, 69–83. New York: Routledge.

Rorty, Richard. 1998. *Achieving Our Country*. Cambridge, Mass.: Harvard University Press.

———. 1991. *Objectivity, Relativism, and Truth*. New York: Cambridge University Press.

Rosenstone, Steven J., and Mark Hansen. 1993. *Mobilization, Participation and Democracy in America*. New York: Macmillan.

Rousseau, Jean-Jacques. 1960 [1758]. *Politics and the Arts*, translated by Allan Bloom. Ithaca, N.Y.: Cornell University Press.

———. 1997 [1762]. *The Social Contract*, translated by Victor Gourevitch. In *The Social Contract and other Later Political Writings*, edited by Victor Gourevitch. New York: Cambridge University Press.

Rubens, Jim. 1983. "Retooling American Democracy." *The Futurist* 17(1): 59–64.

Sachs, Hiram. 1995. "Computer Networks and the Formation of Public Opinion: An Ethnographic Study." *Media, Culture & Society* 17: 81–99.

Schement, Jorge R. 1993. *Beyond Universal Service: Characteristics of Americans Without Telephones, 1980-1993*. Communications Policy Working Paper no.1. Washington, D.C.: The Benton Foundation. Available: http//www.benton.org/Library/Universal/Working1/working1.html.

Schement, Jorge R., and Terry Curtis. 1995. *Tendencies and Tensions of the Information Age: The Production and Distribution of Information in the United States*. New Brunswick, N.J.: Transaction.

Schiller, Herbert I. 1996. *Information Inequality: The Deepening Social Crisis in America*. New York: Routledge.

———. 1989. *Culture, Inc.: The Corporate Takeover of Public Expression*. New York: Oxford University Press.

Schneider, Steven M. 1996. "Creating a Democratic Public Sphere through Political Discussion." *Social Science Computer Review* 14(4): 373–93.

Schön, Donald A., Bish Sanyal, and William J. Mitchell, editors. 1999. *High Technology and Low-Income Communities: Prospects for the Positive Use of Advanced Information Technology*. Cambridge, Mass.: MIT Press.

Schudson, Michael. 1997. "Why Conversation Is Not the Soul of Democracy." *Critical Studies in Mass Communication* 14: 297–309.

Schuler, Douglas. 1996. *New Community Networks: Wired for Change*. New York: ACM Press/Addison-Wesley.

Schumpeter, Joseph A. 1975 [1942]. *Capitalism, Socialism, and Democracy*. New York: Harper.

Schwartzman, Andrew J. 1997. Transcript of panel presentation from Advisory Committee on Public Interest Obligations of Digital Television Broadcasters. Available: http://www.benton.org/PIAC.

Sclove, Richard E. 1995. *Democracy and Technology*. New York: Guilford.

Sellars, Charles. 1991. *The Market Revolution: Jacksonian America, 1815-1846*. New York: Oxford University Press.

**REFERENCES**

Sen, Amartya. 1992. *Inequality Reexamined*. New York: Sage.

Shapiro, Andrew L. 1999. *The Control Revolution: How the Internet Is Putting Individuals in Charge and Changing the World We Know*. New York: A Century Foundation Book.

Sheekey, Arthur. 1997. *Education and Telecommunications: Critical Issues and Resources*. Boston: Information Gatekeeper.

Shenk, David. 1997. *Data Smog: Surviving the Information Glut*. New York: HarperCollins.

Smith, Adam. 1993 [1776]. *An Inquiry into the Nature and Causes of the Wealth of Nations*, edited by Kathryn Sutherland. Oxford: Oxford University Press.

Somerset-Ward, Richard. 1997. *Multiple Services: Programming for the Digital Future*. Washington, D.C.: Corporation for Public Broadcasting.

Soros, George. 1998. *The Crisis of Global Capitalism: Open Society Endangered*. New York: BBS/PublicAffairs.

Spears, Russell, and Martin Lea. 1994. "Panacea or Panopticon? The Hidden Power in Computer-Mediated Communication." *Communication Research* 21: 427–59.

Spertus, Ellen. 1991. "Why Are There So Few Female Computer Scientists?" Cambridge, Mass.: MIT Artificial Intelligence Laboratory.

Sproull, Lee, and Samer Faraj. 1995. "Atheism, Sex, and Databases: The Net as a Social Technology." In *Public Access to the Internet*, edited by Brian Kahin and James Keller, 62–81. Cambridge, Mass.: MIT Press.

Stallabrass, Julian. 1995. "Empowering Technology: The Exploration of Cyberspace." *New Left Review* 211: 3–32.

Stone, Philip J., et al. 1966. *The General Inquirer: A Computer Approach to Content Analysis*. Cambridge, Mass.: MIT Press.

Streck, John. 1998. "Pulling the Plug on Electronic Town Meetings: Participatory Democracy and the Reality of the Usenet." In *The Politics of Cyberspace*, edited by Chris Toulouse and Timothy W. Luke, 18–47. New York: Routledge.

Tambini, Damian. 1998. "Civic Networking and Universal Rights to Connectivity: Bologna." In *Cyberdemocracy: Technology, Cities and Civic Networks*, edited by Roza Tsagarousianou, Damian Tambini, and Cathy Bryan, 84–109. London: Routledge.

Taylor, John, Christine Bellamy, Charles Raab, William H. Dutton, and Malcolm Peltu. 1996. "The Information Polity: Electronic Democracy, Privacy, and Surveillance." In *Information and Communication Technologies: Visions and Realities*, edited by William H. Dutton, 265–82. Oxford: Oxford University Press.

Taylor, Mark C., and Esa Saarinen. 1994. *Imagologies: Media Philosophy*. New York: Routledge.

"Technorealism overview." 1998. Available: http://www.technorealism.org.

Teer-Tomaselli, Ruth. 1996. "The Public Broadcaster and Democracy in Transformation." The 1996 Spry Memorial Lecture. Available: http://www.fas.umontreal.ca/COM/spry/spry-rt-lec.html.

Third International Mathematics and Science Study. 1997. National Center for Education Statistics. Available: http://www.ed.gov/NCES/timss/.

Thoreau, Henry David. 1985 [1854]. *Walden; or, Life in the Woods*. New York: Library of America.

Toffler, Alvin. 1970. *Future Shock*. New York: Random House.

Tsagarousianou, Roza. 1998. "Electronic Democracy and the Public Sphere: Opportunities and Challenges." In *Cyberdemocracy: Technology, Cities and Civic Networks*, edited by Roza Tsagarousianou, Damian Tambini, and Cathy Bryan, 167–78. London: Routledge.

Tsagarousianou, Roza, Damian Tambini, and Cathy Bryan, editors. 1998. *Cyberdemocracy: Technology, Cities and Civic Networks*. London: Routledge.

Turkle, Sherry. 1988, "Computational Reticence: Why Women Fear the Intimate Machine." In *Technology and Women's Voices: Keeping in Touch*, edited by Cheris Kramarae, 41–61. New York: Pergamon.

Turow, Joseph. 1999. *The Internet and the Family: The View from Parents, the View from the Press*, report no. 27. Philadelphia: Annenberg Public Policy Center of the University of Pennsylvania.

U.S. Advisory Council on the National Information Infrastructure. 1996 *Kickstart Initiative*. Washington, D.C.: U.S. Government Printing Office.

U.S. Department of Commerce. 1999. *Falling through the Net: A Report on the Telecommunications and Information Technology Gap in America*. Washington, D.C.: U.S. Department of Commerce.

————. 1996. *Lessons Learned from the Telecommunications and Information Infrastructure Assistance Program*. Washington D.C.: U.S. Department of Commerce.

U.S. Department of Education. Office of Educational Research and Improvement. 1997. *The Social Context of Education*. Washington, D.C.: National Center for Education Statistics.

U.S. Secretary of Commerce. 1994. *Administration White Paper on Communications Act Reforms*. Washington, D.C.: U.S. Department of Commerce.

Varley, Pamela. 1991. "Electronic Democracy." *Technology Review* 94(8): 43–51.

Verba, Sidney, Kay Lehman Schlozman, and Henry E. Brady. 1995. *Voice and Equality: Civic Voluntarism in American Politics*. Cambridge, Mass.: Harvard University Press.

Verba, Sidney, Kay Lehman Schlozman, Henry Brady, and Norman Nie. 1993. "Race, Ethnicity and Political Resources: Participation in the United States." *British Journal of Political Science* 23: 453–97.

Villa, Dana R. 1996. *Arendt and Heidegger: The Fate of the Political*. Princeton: Princeton University Press.

Volgy, Thomas J., and John E. Schwarz, 1983. "Misreporting and Vicarious Political Participation at the Local Level." *Public Opinion Quarterly* 48: 757–65.

Walsh, Ekaterina O. 1999. "The Digital Melting Pot." The Forrester Brief, March 3. Cambridge, Mass.: Forrester Research, Inc.

Walton, Anthony. 1999. "Technology versus African-Americans." *The Atlantic Monthly* 283(1): 14, 16–8.

Weber, Robert P. 1990. *Basic Content Analysis*. Newbury Park: Sage.

Webster, Frank, and Kevin Robins. 1998. "The Iron Cage of the Information Society." *Information, Communication & Society* 1(1): 23–45.

Weeks, Edward C., Margaret Hallock, James B. Lemert, and Bruce McKinlay. 1992. *Citizen Participation in Policy Formation: A Review of Governor Roberts' Conversation with Oregon*. Eugene: University of Oregon.

**REFERENCES**

Werbach, Kevin. 1999 *The Architecture of the Internet 2.0.* Available: http://www.edventure.com/release1/cable.html.

White House Press Release. 1998. "Statement by Vice President Gore on E-Rate Applications for Schools and Libraries," April 22. Available: http//www.whitehouse.gov/WH.html/library.html.

White, John J. 1990. *Literary Futurism: Aspects of the First Avant Garde.* Oxford: Clarendon Press.

Wilhelm, Anthony G. 1998a. *Closing the Digital Divide: Enhancing Hispanic Participation in the Information Age.* Claremont, Calif.: The Tomás Rivera Policy Institute.

———. 1998b. "Buying into the Computer Age: A Look at Hispanic Families." In *Proceedings of the Families, Technology, and Education Conference,* edited by Anne S. Robertson. Champaign, Ill.: ERIC Clearinghouse on Elementary and Early Childhood Education, National Parent Information Network.

———. 1996. "Creative Destruction in the Information Age: The Fallout on America's Latino Communities." *Trotter Review* 9(2): 14–8.

Williams, Frederick, and Susan Hadden. 1992. "On the Prospects for Redefining Universal Service: From Connectivity to Content." In *Between Communication and Information,* edited by Jorge R. Schement and Brent D. Ruben, 401–19. New Brunswick: Transaction.

Williams, Robin, and David Edge . 1996. "The Social Shaping of Technology." In *Information and Communication Technologies: Visions and Realities,* edited by William H. Dutton, 53–67. New York: Oxford University Press.

Wilson, William J. 1996. *When Work Disappears: The World of the New Urban Poor.* New York: Alfred A. Knopf.

Winner, Langdon. 1998. "The Real Millennium Bug," *Tech Knowledge Revue,* September 9. Available: http://www.rpi.edu/~winner/techknow.html.

World Institute on Disability. 1994. *Building the Framework: Telecommunications and Persons with Disabilities.* Available: http://www.igc.org.

Yzerbyt, Vincent, Jacques-Phillipe Leyens, and Fanny Bellour. 1995. "The Ingroup Overexclusion Effect: Identity Concerns in Discussion about Group Membership." *European Journal of Social Psychology* 25: 239–50.

# INDEX